Justice Forgetaboutit

Justice Forgetaboutit

A TRUE STORY OF ONE MAN'S PURSUIT FOR
JUSTICE WITHIN A CORRUPT JUDICIAL SYSTEM

Robert J. Mammola

Copyright © 2016 Robert J. Mammola
All rights reserved.

ISBN: 153710554X
ISBN 13: 9781537105543
Library of Congress Control Number: 2016913515
CreateSpace Independent Publishing Platform
North Charleston, South Carolina

Justice

Forgetaboutit

Boston, Massachusetts, bankruptcy court under Chapter 11 reorganization—tyranny, usurpation, despotism, insolence, nepotism, and impunity laid out in motions filed as court documents.

Absolute Denial of Due Process

All men are created equal, that they are endowed by their Creator with certain unalienable Rights…

—US Declaration of Independence

Author's Note

In East Cambridge, Massachusetts, where I was born and lived for the first thirteen years of my life, when you said thank you to someone who did something for you or made a good gesture, inevitably, that person would respond, "Forget about it!" A note to the backstabbing saboteurs in this true story, this is street justice, legally, no hiding behind closed doors.

Street justice is face to face anywhere anytime.

Welcome to my world.

I personally want to thank my readers for their support.

Sincerely,

Robert Joseph Mammola

Preface

The Story you are about to embark on is a very difficult yet factual documentary and educational chain of events, injustices, and criminal actions committed by the very people who took an oath or passed the bar to defend and protect the US Constitution in the pursuit of justice in the US Bankruptcy Court in Boston, Massachusetts. A particular judge's actions coupled with rulings that went way beyond misconduct; they actually border on tyranny. The bankruptcy judge, a less than honest trustee, the judge's former law partner, and another less than honest and incompetent trustee have violated and discarded every law they swore to uphold. All of these injustices were in the form of motions filed in court. Under the pains and penalties of perjury, I stand behind every statement in this story; they are backed up with court documentation. My family and I had a very successful real estate business for over twenty-three years. We were in the process of selling off our real estate as condos at the time that the real estate market—unbeknown to the general public—was headed into a serious meltdown (2008). Our bank for more than five years, Mount Washington Bank, located in South Boston, led us to believe that they were going to refinance all of our mortgages at a lower interest rate. The less-than-honest CEO, Ed Merrit, personally asked me to take over a family member's mortgage to help the bank out. The CEO stated the bank would pay all the closing costs and work into the mortgage any back real estate taxes owed when all the refinancing was done. Unbeknown to my family, Mount Washington Bank was in the middle of a serious FDIC investigation. The investigation was in regard to bad banking practices, and they were in the process of having a banking consultant run the bank until a merger between Mount Washington Bank and East Boston Savings Bank was completed. In a press release, the two Boston banks made it look like the merger was a great move for both banks. The CEO of Mount Washington Bank never told us that the bank was in trouble with the FDIC and was in no position to refinance, nor were they allowed to per the FDIC order. He was just being deceitful in regard to any refinancing of all our property. That was a con to get the loan to Robert Joseph Mammola (R.J.M.), a nonperforming loan, off the books and to mislead the FDIC investigators. That was when Mount Washington Bank and East Boston Savings Bank started their deceitful plot to survive, and my family, the Mammolas, got dragged into their plot to destroy their customers in order for both banks to survive. That was the beginning of this horrifying but true story.

The Beginning

The names in this factual and educational documentation of vicious, deliberate, destructive greed and retaliation against a law-abiding Family will be those of the actual people who to date have been successful in playing out their scheme of artifice.

I, Robert Joseph Mammola, in the year 1994 was forty-eight years old (not young). I was just recovering from my first heart procedure to correct the rhythm of my heart, as I was suffering from atrial fibrillation. It was straightened out at that point, thank God, but for two years after the procedure, I was unable to work. I am thankful I progressively got stronger and was able to go back to work in 1994.

My profession was a master electrician and HVAC mechanic, and I had been in business for myself some twenty-five years at that point in time. Through my business, I started to buy income property. In light of my heart condition, I decided to put all the property in realty trusts for my wife and three children. Each of them would own 25 percent of each trust. A realty trust is a legal document that explains who owns which share of the trust, while the trust owns the real estate. I did this to ensure their future. Section 5 of the trust explicitly requires all the beneficiaries' written approval to do anything with the trust. So my wife and daughters gave me power of attorney, enabling me to manage the property and run the businesses. It allowed me to make leases and loans, maintain the property, and collect the rents. I was always looking for other property to buy and secure financing for, even though I did not own any of the property. Because of my credit and my business background, the banks wanted me to personally guarantee all loans, which I did. The judge, trustees, attorneys, and the Boston banks had no idea they were climbing into bed with the devil himself. This is what I become if somebody crosses or abuses me. They didn't know where Robert J. Mammola was raised and who his parents were.

My father and mother were the greatest parents. I am the seventh born of eight children, two girls and six boys. We were brought up to be very respectful, honest, and devout Christians. With this background, my parents were committed to preparing us to stay together no matter what. We were taught to never, ever let anyone abuse any of us. I was born and raised in East Cambridge, Massachusetts, on the wrong side of the tracks, as the saying goes, for which I am very grateful. I learned early that to survive I had to fight constantly and had to be street smart. When I was thirteen, my parents bought a house in Lexington, MA. This was a great move for my younger brother and me. We were both very fortunate to have had the opportunity to complete our education in a highly accredited school system.

The true beginning of this story was in 2008, when the real estate market was in a meltdown. Nobody knew what disaster lay ahead. In July of 1994, the trust bought property in Malden, Massachusetts, on Main Street. The property consisted of twelve commercial storefronts, a single-family home, a two-family home, and a four-family home. The property was two houses short of a city block in the center of Malden. We formed our first trust, called Triple M Realty Trust.

In December of 1994, we bought 10 Yeamans Street in Revere, Massachusetts. There we formed another trust called Ten Yeamans Street Trust. That property was located on the corner of Broadway and Yeamans Street. That particular property consisted of twenty-six apartments and five commercial storefronts, located on the Broadway side. Next, in the year 2004, we bought a property located at 14 Yeamans Street. For this property, we created another trust, called the Fourteen Yeamans Street Trust. This property consisted of a three-family house with enough parking for twelve cars.

We renovated all these properties, and to do that, I borrowed government funds administered by the North Shore Consortium in these amounts: for Malden, $350,000, and for Revere, $278,000. To qualify, we had to commit 10 percent of the units to low-income housing. We had ten years to pay back these loans, and we paid them in five.

My family had just finished converting the Revere property into condos—a three-family and mixed unit complex with twenty-six apartments and five storefronts.

In December of 2006, I bailed out my brother and his family by getting a mortgage in my name for the property known as Meyer Road in Hamilton, Massachusetts.

My courage, conviction, resolve, and, most important, my Christian faith were insurmountable.

In 2008, the CEO of the Boston bank used by my family came to me and asked me to help the bank with the mortgage payments owed by my daughter and son-in-law. They were behind. This property was at 10 Milano Avenue in Revere.

At this time, we were in the process of refinancing the three trusts held by my wife and daughters as well as the Hamilton property, which was in my name. The lower interest rates on refinancing would reduce our monthly payments between four and five thousand a month. This would make it possible for me to take over the mortgage on the Milano Avenue property in my own name.

The CEO was very appreciative of my decision. Sometime later, he thanked me publicly at a breakfast function at the JFK Library.

That troubled property—Milano Avenue—closed in November of 2008 and was transferred to me personally. The mortgage was for $401,000 at 5 percent interest, but the property appraised at $310,000. The appraisal and closing costs were paid by the bank. The Boston bank asked me to roll the back real estate taxes owed on Milano Avenue—$4,400—until the refinancing of all the families' mortgages. I agreed. This action saved the bank over ninety thousand dollars. I did not know how much the CEO and the Boston bank appreciated my taking over Milano Avenue. I understood this afterward when the bank came under investigation by the FDIC and the running of the bank had been turned over to a consultant in the summer of 2009, per the FDIC order.

If I had known beforehand, in November of 2008, that the bank was in trouble, I would not have taken over the Milano Avenue mortgage. And furthermore I would have refinanced with HUD on all our properties. I still have the documentation regarding HUD's loan commitment. It wasn't until later that we saw a press release stating that the CEO of my Mount Washington Bank [MT/WB] and the CEO of the East Boston Savings bank [EBSB] had met in April 2008 to start talking about the framework of a merger. EBSB was planning to take over the MT/WB. All this time and at the time of the Milano Avenue transaction, my family had no idea that the FDIC was investigating our bank for bad and improper banking practices or forcing that bank into a merger with a EBSB.

In the spring of 2009, the vice president who handled all the accounts called a meeting regarding the refinancing of my property and the property of my wife and daughters.

At this time, the FDIC made the bank bring in a consultant to get the bank on track. We will politely call him "Mr. B." Mr. B. may have been qualified as a consultant, but he did a very poor job. Mr. B. got in the middle of the completion of the refinancing negotiations. The vice president, Mr. B., and I went over all the trust records. Mr. B. said the records and the cash flow were very good. The bank would put a package together, and the vice president would get back to me.

After leaving the meeting, I called the CEO of my bank to ask why he had not been at that meeting. He said that Mr. B. was a good man and knew how important the Mammola family was to the bank. A week later, the vice president called to set another meeting to view all the properties: he, Mr. B., and I met in Malden, Massachusetts. Mr. B. stepped into three of the storefronts, just in and out. It was clear that he had no interest at all. It was just a show.

Then he said, "Let's see Revere," and I asked about the other twenty-three units at Malden. He wasn't interested. He just wanted to go to Revere. There, he did the same—in and out of two storefronts—and then he said, "Let's go back to Malden."

I said, "There are three condo units to look at right here," but he insisted on going back to Malden. I asked about seeing Milano Avenue while we were in Revere.

He said, "No. I'm all set."

Then I asked about the property in Hamilton, and he still insisted on going back to Malden. At this point, it was very hard not give this inept, arrogant excuse for a businessman a well-deserved East Cambridge beating. I could taste it.

Not much was said during the seven minutes it took to get back to Malden. But to me, it was a long, long trip. It didn't take a genius to know that nothing good was coming of this meeting. I truly wish I had kicked his brains—what little he might have had—all over the Malden parking lot. The time in jail would have been a cakewalk compared to what my family has been put through. I heard once that what goes around always comes around. When we arrived in Malden, the wannabe consultant turned to me and said, "I can tell you now the bank will do nothing unless you take your two properties and the three trust properties and cross-collateralize them." This means that one loan is dependent on the others. If one fails, they are all in default. The advantage to the bank in doing this is that all the equity in all those properties is subject to each loan individually and collectively. If one loan defaulted, the bank could foreclose on all the properties.

My reply was, "I can't do that. The Milano Avenue and Hamilton properties are mine, but the three trust properties belong to my wife and daughters."

Mr. B.'s reply was that the bank would have to then foreclose on all three trusts for back taxes. These back taxes were for converting the three trust properties into condominiums, which tripled the tax bill on each condo before even one had been sold. Usually these taxes would be paid as the condos were sold. But because the bank wanted to cross-collateralize, they were using this as a threat.

I turned to the vice president of the bank and asked, "What's going on here?"

He had no answer.

Mr. B. said, "You're dealing with me."

I asked the vice president, "Does the CEO of the bank know about this?"

Mr. B. said, "Did you hear me? You're dealing with me."

I politely tried to tell him to shut his fucking big mouth or I would give him a backhand. He did shut up, and he got out of my truck. The vice president said he was sorry. It was out of his control.

Mr. B., that piece of work, knew I had other banks that wanted my family's business. Our monthly mortgage payments were $23,000, which was automatically withdrawn every month. (Remember, this story is all backed up with documents.) What did that rat, Mr. B., do? He had the vice president in the credit department report our payments two months in arrears. That stopped any bank from refinancing us and was done to force us into cross-collateralizing all the properties. A new bank would have enabled the girls to pay all the back taxes and sewer and water liens, plus penalties—approximately $250,000. Most of this would have been paid when the condos were sold. At this point, the false credit report gave us a giant black eye in terms of refinancing. Remember, Mr. B. was put into the bank with a mission to shore up the bank's collateral position. One of the most important parts of the FDIC order was for the bank, through a competent consultant, to cross-collateralize every loan over $750,000. The FDIC order gave the bank a ninety-day window to have this done. That window ended at the end of October 2009. These are parts of the FDIC cease-and-desist order:

1. no more bad business practices
2. no more operating with an inadequate level of capital
3. no more operating without adequate supervision

My family had no choice but to call our attorney to work on the false credit report. At this time, neither we nor any of the other bank customers were aware of the FDIC order.

Our attorney questioned the bank regarding the inaccuracies of the credit report. The bank replied that they had inadvertently misapplied the funds. (The funds were there.) The new mortgage company told me to have the bank e-mail the information about the mistake, and the credit bureau would remove it within twenty-four hours. The Boston bank refused, saying they would have it removed within three weeks, as the law allowed them thirty days. In the meantime, my family lost the mortgage commitment. The bank's attorney and Mr. B. sent an e-mail to our attorney stating that if I, Robert Mammola, did not cross-collateralize as proposed by the bank by October 7, 2009, the bank would commence foreclosure and litigation against us.

On October 5, 2009, my wife and I filed a lawsuit against the MT/WB in superior court. After filing our lawsuit, through what's called discovery, our attorney found out exactly how deceitful the CEO of the bank, the bank's employees, the wannabe consultant, and the CEO of the EBSB bank had been. In press releases, both my Boston bank's CEO and the CEO of the EBSB bank made it look like their merger was their own great idea when, in fact, it was a forced merger. For reasons laid out in the FDIC investigation, my Boston bank was required to bring in a stronger bank in order to survive. Remember, this is the bank that asked for my help with the mortgage for Milano Avenue in Revere. They had desperately needed me to help them look good with the FDIC, regarding problem loans.

Talking about looking good! The lifesaving EBSB and MT/WB had put out a press release on July 20, 2009, stating, among other things, that they had played by the rules and done everything right. They claimed not to have set people up for failure in the way that larger banks were doing. "We," they said, "stuck to our principals and did things the right way." They claimed they were cognizant of the needs of their customers.

What they left out while telling the public just how honest and wonderful they were in signing the merger was that it was a forced merger. The smaller MT/WB, my bank, signed the FDIC order to cease and desist, and the CEO of EBSB was most deceitful. It turned out he was an army buddy of my cousin. At a family gathering that took place around this time, my oldest daughter, Di and my cousin Albie were talking when the CEO's name came up. Di yelled out, "Papa, get over here! Hurry." She said, "Papa, you're not going to believe who cousin Albie's army buddy is."

I asked, "Who?"

And Al replied, "The CEO of the Boston takeover bank."

I was blown away. We talked for about half an hour.

Al said, "I'll call him," and he did. They talked for a couple of minutes, and then Al gave me the phone.

We greeted each other, and the CEO asked what was going on. I explained the problems the consultant had caused, and the CEO said, "They have not taken control as yet."

For the time being, he wanted me to make sure I got the current appraisals that my Boston bank was having done. This my attorney subsequently did. The CEO suggested that once he was in control, he could make things right. But when he did get control, I called, but he would not respond. He has also stopped talking to my cousin Al. As the reader follows the story it will be very clear that Gavegnano the C.E.O. of East Boston Savings Bank. Does not know the difference between Cognizant and a Vendetta.

By this time, we were in superior court. The first two hearings were in front of an African-American judge who was not going to let the bank's attorney skirt the law. This judge was only interested in the facts of the suit to secure justice.

The bank's attorney waved trust beneficiary certificates around while walking around the courtroom, stating the bank did not know who owned the property and whether we were lying or committing fraud.

Then he presented to the court a document stating that my wife and I were the beneficiaries. Since the trust was in the names of my daughters and my wife and not mine, our attorney, to say the least, was shocked as to this new deceitful surprise documents that the bank supplied their attorneys.

The third time in court before a different judge, our attorney presented documentation that proved the beneficiary certificates presented to the court by the bank's attorney previously were not, in fact, the real ones (and were not recorded at the registry of deeds from the closing). The judge was looking out the window. He had no interest in the documentation that our attorney was presenting to the court.

My family had, on a monthly basis, at that point, paid the MT/WB almost a total $1,400,000 in mortgage payments. (That must leave fraud out.) The documentation that our attorney filed was an affidavit from another attorney my family used for leases and evictions. He had received an e-mail from MT/WB's closing attorney, asking for assistance on a new loan back in 2004. He had stated, at that time, that my wife and I, Robert and Seta Mammola, were the beneficiaries of the trust, but in his affidavit, he admitted this had been a mistake on his part.

Also supplied to the court, documents from the bank's financial adviser, dated 2007, stated that I, Robert J. Mammola, did not own any of the property in all three trusts and my wife and three daughters had equal shares of 25 percent each. The judge gave these documents no credence. These incorrect beneficiary certificates were never filed at the registry of deeds. Only the accurate and originals were. To keep this story factual and honest, we signed the mistaken documents at three loan closings. I, as the one with all the experience, should have seen the error. This is not an excuse, but it was a very casual transaction. The bank's vice president and I became very friendly. We also did not have an attorney present. The closings were simple refinancing of existing loans from another bank at a better interest rate. After a couple of appeals in superior court were denied, we appealed to the appeals court. That was going to take some time—time we did not have. I was forced to file bankruptcy, Chapter 7 liquidation, in July 2010 on the property in Revere at 10 Milano Avenue (the same property that the CEO of my bank ten months earlier had asked me to help with, saving the bank some $90,000, as stated in the minutes of the bank). My Hamilton property was foreclosed on in my filing. I must make it very clear that none of my mortgages and none of my wife's or daughters' mortgages were late or behind in any payments. My wife, as trustee of the three trusts, had to file Chapter

11 bankruptcy reorganization on May 10, 2010. As a family, we made a very hard business decision to sell our best piece of property in Malden, Massachusetts, which consisted of a One single family unit, a two family, four family, three condo apartments above twelve store fronts, and a three car garage, three condo apartments, twelve storefronts, and a three-car garage. The condos broke down into twenty-three units, which could be sold as is. Plans and condo documents were completed. Five of the existing tenants gave deposits to purchase the units they presently occupied. The average sale price per unit was $200,000. Another long-term tenant, a charitable organization of twenty-five years that feeds over thirty thousand people per year was negotiating with my family to buy two units with us holding their mortgage. This charitable organization had been our tenants since 1994 with no rent increases.

We hired Century 21 of Malden, Massachusetts, to help sell the remaining as condos units. Under our agreement, the single-family unit were to be sold for $200,000, the two-family ones for $325,000, the minimarket for $300,000, the Ethiopian restaurant for $275,000, and the Indian market for $220,000—a total $1,370,000. That was with only five units, sales for a mortgage of $1,170,000. The charitable organization sale is not included in the total sales, because we were going to hold the mortgage of $425,000 minus their deposit. They were in the process of raising money for the deposit. Other existing tenants were looking for financing. When twenty-three units had been completely sold, a total of $4,650,000 would have been realized. Malden's existing mortgage was $1,170,000. The Malden and Revere taxes and liens were $250,000. The total owed was $1,420,000. The balance would be $3,180,000, minus credit-card debt of $80,000, mostly business bills from condo renovations. My family's profit would be $3,000,000. I called each of the credit-card banks and companies and told them my family had filed Chapter 11 and that we had put our best property on the market. When it sold, they would be paid in full. Not one of them harassed us. They just waited. They knew from our past history of payments they would be paid. The Chapter 11 reorganization was going into its sixth month, and my daughter was doing all the monthly operating reports as the court-appointed property manager without any problems or complaints from the US trustee who received them every month. This trustee was also the US trustee who held the 341 meeting, "regarding the debtor S. R. Mammola's plans to reorganize her financial affairs." The broker was showing the units that were not under agreement with existing tenants that had deposits. All was going as my wife and daughter e had laid out at the 341 meeting. At that meeting, my daughter became the court-appointed property manager.

Suddenly, the judge appointed a trustee on October 4, 2010 (sua sponte). By federal law, the US trustees' office is in charge of appointing a trustee but only if there is just cause. There was none. On October 13, 2010, my Chapter 7 trustee filed a motion of appearance in the Chapter 11 case. My property was released to the bank to foreclose on. My daughter and I met with the chapter 11 trustee. She made an appointment with Diane and me at her office on Saturday morning. My wife, the debtor, was to be there but was ill. For the next two weeks, Diane and I went over the functions of all the trust properties. We supplied the trustee with all the condo plans and condo documents, as well as the five offers to purchase from existing tenants. We gave the trustee the contract that the S. R. M. trustee of all three trusts signed with the Century 21 Real Estate agent in July 2010. In addition, the Seta R. Mammola trustee supplied a letter from a finance LLC group that stated they would refinance her in the amount of $2,300,000 at 10 percent, the financing acquired through Seta R. Mammola's court-appointed accountants on September 27, 2010. This loan was arranged by her bankruptcy attorney and the bankruptcy accountants. Seta R. Mammola, as the debtor in possession under the federal Reform Act of 1978, could secure new financing to reorganize (referred to as a super priority lien). It all looked good, and the court trustee was pleased with what had been accomplished in the short time of her filing on May 2010 just six months earlier. In a few weeks, the trustee's attitude changed. Her position was that the Malden property had to be sold as a package. We had no idea why she changed from the condo plan to a package sale. This was not the best way. The property would sell for half its value, as we told the court-appointed trustee.

The trust trustee came to the next meeting to tell the court-appointed trustee that was not what she as trustee of the family trusts wanted. The trustee told the court-appointed trustee that five of the existing tenants had given deposits, the broker at Century 21 had lots of other buyers, and her husband was working on the purchase of two more units with the Bread of Life a charitable organization. They had been tenants for almost twenty years. Now the cat was out of the bag. The court trustee made it very clear that—in her words—we had bigger problems. That the Chapter 7 trustee was demanding a $250,000 payment due to me as a 50 percent owner of all three trusts. Seta said, "That's BS. My husband is not an owner, and if that ass of a seven trustee wants to screw around, I want a hearing with the judge. Our trust documents were made up by the best attorney in Boston. My husband had hours of a deposition with all our factual trust documentation with his seven trustee. That trustee can't just change the facts. That's why we must have a court hearing."

The court trustee replied, "If you try anything like that, the judge will automatically convert the Chapter 11 to a Chapter 7 liquidation and you will lose all your property."

The judge and the Chapter 7 trustee were close friends and former partners.

Seta went to her Chapter 11 attorney regarding a court hearing. He said, "I'm trying to work out a deal to settle for $10,000 to get this problem behind us. The judge in a situation like this has a judicial responsibility to pursue justice as the oath of office requires." (In part, the oath reads, "I take this obligation freely, without any mental reservation or purpose of evasion.")

I watched the Chapter 7 trustee run the judge's courtroom and conspire to lay out his plan of fraud and deception to sabotage our family's real estate business and future for his greed. This was on the verge of pushing me out of control. I made up my mind; I would learn and do whatever it took to destroy all of them. I watched the judge allow the Chapter 7 trustee (her former partner in a law firm) file motion after motion of deceit and boldface lies without any questions and then deny each and every motion or appeal that I made. At that point, she was not being a judge in the pursuit of justice.

It became very clear to me how I was going to bring the whole group of them down—the judge, the trustees, their attorneys, the banks, and their attorneys—by using the very system they swore to support and defend (the supreme law of the land), the Constitution of the United States of America. I bought every book on the Constitution. After I read it about twenty times, it started to sink in. The judge, trustees, and attorneys were breaking every one of the first ten amendments (the Bill of Rights) and every federal rule. It was very clear the Chapter 7 trustee had the Chapter 11 trustee appointed by the judge sua sponte. If the US trustee made the appointment, by rules of the Reform Act of 1978, the US trustee must make sure the appointed trustee is qualified, knowledgeable, and competent. That leaves the judge's sua sponte appointed trustee out. You can forget about the Chapter 11 trustee's competence. Just listen to the audiotapes of the court hearing. Listen to the judge's tone of irritation while the trustee is trying to make a point. The judge is obviously saying, "Where did she come from?" Oops, I mean, tyrant, sua sponte, remember? A competent trustee, appointed by the US trustee would not have been under the Chapter 7 trustee's control, her former partner, and would not have violated Federal Rule Section 157 (in part) to "devise a scheme or artifice to defraud" or allow Federal Rule subsection 704 (5) (in part) if a purpose would be served, and examine proofs of claims and object to the allowance of any claim that was improper, which could not have happened. The Chapter 7 trustee's, his attorney's, and his law firm's conspiracy scheme would not have been able to be played out. The reader, by now, knows the Mammolas were on the attack. The *judge*, trustees, attorneys, and the two Boston banks were about to learn they were not above the *law*.

I then began having my daughter search the web regarding bankruptcy laws and (federal laws). Low and behold, they had even less regard for them. Needless to say, I couldn't wait to dissect all the motions that had been filed. Mostly, I couldn't wait for more deceit and deception to be filed. The conspiracy now had a mind of its own. Both trustees, their attorneys, and their law firms were now just out to build a massive case for billing hours (filled with lies and deception and under the pains and penalty of perjury). My Chapter 7 trustee thought he was just the best. At his office, there was a pause in my deposition, I was asked to wait in the lobby for a few minutes. Mr. Big Short (the Chapter 7 trustee) couldn't help himself. While he was wiping his hands, standing with two secretaries, he said, "Is my attorney taking good care of you, Mr. Mammola?"

I just looked at him. The hairs in the back of my head stood up. Remember, I am a streetfighter. The East Cambridge in me wanted to wipe that phony smile off that snake's ugly face. But I knew I was being set up. I had to be quiet for the time being. As it turned out, not one thing in my deposition was reported truthfully in his attorney's motion of overwhelming evidence of facts that I was a 50 percent owner of all three realty trusts. Remember, the judge was this attorney's boss's former partner. He knew he could say anything, true or not, and the judge was not going to check if it was factual or not. She didn't.

Some of their overwhelming evidence was the following

>They said I formed a trust in 1988 and put my wife, S.R.M., as trustee, and my daughter Michela and my wife as beneficiaries and owners of the trust (March 1988). (I met my wife in September of 1988. We were married on May 21, 1989. Our daughter Michela was born August 4, 1990.)
>
>The Chapter 7 trustee's attorney stated (factually) that I treated the trust as my own. Remember, at my deposition supplied all factual documentation. One piece was a document giving me power of attorney for all three trusts signed by all the beneficiaries. This was done in keeping with the rules of a trust.

These are just two of the Chapter 7 trustee's deceitful ways to give the judge an excuse for her unlawful court rulings. Little did she (the judge or her former partner, the Chapter 7 trustee) realize that we were documenting every violation of the supreme law of the land, the Constitution—every article, every amendment, and every federal law they criminally violated over greed for money, in the process destroying an entire family, emotionally and financially unbeknown to them, to their detriment. The judge, who took an oath to support and defend the Constitution of the United States, must have forgotten the *Fourteenth Amendment*—in part (no state may take away any person's life, liberty, or property without proper operation of the law or abridge the citizen's privileges or immunities. They belligerently violated and abused this amendment by their abuse of power (in the Constitution, the framers called it abuse of power or usurpation). The judge used the trustee's attorney's motion of lies to deny me my constitutional rights (due process of law). I filed a motion for the clarification and declaratory relief; the federal law requires a jury trial as to the facts. The judge denied it (stating, "I will take no action on this motion") based on her former partner's motion of deceit and lies and because my motion was procedurally wrong. The judge must have forgotten the Fourteenth Amendment of the Constitution, which was adopted in 1868. The Fourteenth Amendment substantiates the doctrine of substantive due process clause, which not only requires due process—that is, basic procedural right—but also protects basic substantive rights. Substantive rights are those general rights that reserve to the individual the power to possess or to do certain things (despite the government's desire to the contrary). These are rights like freedom of speech and religion. "Procedural" rights are special rights that instead dictate how the government can lawfully go about taking away a any person's life, liberty, or property. However, under substantive due process, the Supreme Court has developed a broader interpretation of the clause, one that protects basic substantive rights, as well as the right to process. Substantive due process holds that the due process clause of the Fifth and Fourteenth Amendments guarantee not only that appropriate and just procedures (or "processes") be used whenever the Government is punishing a person or otherwise taking away a person's life, freedom, or property, but that these clauses also guarantee that a person's life, freedom, and property cannot be taken without appropriate governmental justification, regardless of the procedures used to do the taking. In a sense, it makes the due process clause a due substance clause as well. She also solemnly swore (or affirmed) that she would support and defend the Constitution of the United States against all enemies foreign and domestic and that she took this obligation freely without any mental reservation or purpose of evasion so help her God. The trustees, both the Chapter 7 and 11, must have missed Federal Rule 11 U.S.C Subsection (a). Finally, rule 28 USC subsection 959 provides that (in part) trustees may be sued, without leave of the court appointing them. Also they shall not deprive a litigant of his or her right to a trial by jury.

There is also the Barton Doctrine "exception" [Ultra Viries] when a trustee wrongfully seizes possession of a third party's assets. Property, not assets of the estate, may be sued for damages arising out of one's illegal occupation in a state court without leave of the appointing court.

Thomas Jefferson said, in 1778, "Experience hath shewn, that even under the best forms of Government, those entrusted with power have, in time, and by slow Operations, perverted it into Tyranny" (or a tyrant judge, one more important point by R.J.M., 2014).

Article 6.2 of the US Constitution says, in part, that all judges in every state will be bound by this supreme law. My family, at this point, had lost all control of its property and means to financial survival. What do we say to the tenants who had deposits to buy the unit they occupied? Once the trustee (trustee what a joke!) took over, the Chapter 7 trustee said, "Don't lose sight of who's running this conspiracy scheme. Certainly not the Chapter 11 trustee." She was beside herself that she had been put into Chapter 11 within two weeks. She was told, "Just do what you're told." And she did. Another bomb, once she was appointed, the attorney for the debtor Seta R. Mammola was out. He had no say. Remember he was the attorney running all the Chapter 11 court motions and hearings.

He also had the Chapter 11 accountants secure the $2,300,000 loan to refinance our home in Medford and the Triple M. Rt. Trust property in Malden, Massachusetts, which the accountants billed $6,000 for services the Chapter 11 trustee paid out of Seta Mammola's estate but refused to use. This loan was to pay for our home, Triple M., and all the back taxes for Malden and Revere. Here is what they stopped. Let's take the $2,300,000 new financing that the Debtor Seta R. Mammola secured. Triple M. condos in Malden, Massachusetts, twenty-three units, sold for $4,650,000.

The condo property in Malden had a mortgage of $1,170,000.

Taxes owed and liens for Malden and Revere totaled $250,000.

The existing mortgage on 34 Mammola Way was $270,000.

The total balance of Malden sales minus these three is $2,960,000, which would pay back the new financing of $2,300,000.

The total proceeds from the Malden condo sales would be $660,000. Our home, without a mortgage, was valued at $1,000,000. There was no loss of 10 and 14 Yeamans Street income property of $36,000 per month, less mortgage and taxes, for $18,400 per month. Income to the Mammola family was $17,600 per month.

The Supreme (judicial) Court has said that "an act or practice is deceptive if it possesses a tendency to deceive. *Leardi v. Brown,* 366 Mass. 151,156 (1985 Since reliance does not need to be proven, a practice is deceptive if it could reasonably be found to have caused a person to act differently from the way he or she otherwise would have acted." This definition applies to the Chapter 11 trustee's actions while she was under the control of the Chapter 7 trustee's scheme to deceive and sabotage (deliberately destroy) as stated in a motion filed by the Chapter 7 trustee. My family, to say the least, was in a no-win situation. The S.R.M. chapter 11 case would proceed without an attorney. Sorry the Chapter 11 trustee brought in her own law firm to ensure that she wouldn't have any obstacles that would prevent her from following the chapter 7 conspiracy scheme, which she did. She had nobody to answer to other than the Chapter 7 trustee as to his scheme. Remember, we were, in street talk, "clocking" each and every violation, regarding the Constitution and the federal laws that were being totally disregarded. Believe me, they were supplying loads and loads of factual documentation (evidence) for us to use to destroy them at their own game. They thought they were untouchable.

At this point, the Chapter 11 trustee became abusive and arrogant and started giving orders to the real estate broker that Seta Mammola, as trustee, hired to sell Malden property as condos. The broker was told by the Chapter 11 trustee, "You are now working for me, not the Mammolas." What the Chapter 11 trustee forgot was the federal rules, which state that the trustee has a fiduciary obligation to run the debtor's business in the usual way the debtor would (Federal Rule subsection 1106). These are the Chapter 11 trustee's statutory duties. The trustee is an independent third party who "steps into the shoes" of the debtor's management and becomes a fiduciary with an obligation of fairness to all parties in the case. She, the Chapter 11 trustee, was following the rules the chapter 7 trustee laid out with the total approval of the *judge*. If there is any question, as to who was running Seta R. Mammola's chapter 11 case, just remember the Chapter 11 trustee was told not to sell Malden as a package by the debtor whose shoes she stepped into by federal law. Malden would only sell for half as a package, and Seta R. Mammola had five deposits to buy as condos from existing tenants. Remember, the trustee, per Federal Rule 1106, which states the obligation of fairness to all parties in the case. To date (February 25, 2016), some have not received their deposits back. The trustee and the real estate broker, in the broker's words, "decided to gather the utility bills after the closing and pay them." To date (February, 25, 2016), Triple M. Property still owes the national grid over $4,000 for gas and electric. The Chapter 11 trustee has been told about the national grid every time the national grid called my cell phone regarding the bill. The trustee simply ignored that obligation with total disregard to her fiduciary obligation (Federal Rule 1106), stepping into the debtor's shoes. Before the sale, some of the tenants stopped paying their rent so as to recoup their deposits. The Chapter 11 trustee refused to address the tenants as to her change from condos to a package sale. Her statement was "That's not my job."

Two fistfights broke out over the change to a package sale when we were trying to collect rents. The tenants felt that we were going to make more money by selling Triple M. as a package. Potential buyers who had been working with us were convinced they were being pushed aside and out of the way. The karate tenant at 525 Main stopped paying. The Chapter 11 trustee said to Seta R. Mammola, the debtor, "You're not paying attention. I keep telling you we have bigger fish to worry about. That's the Chapter 7 trustee forcing a settlement as to his claim that R.J.M. is a 50 percent owner of all the trust, which the bank's attorney has told him."

At this point, the broker that Seta, the trustee of triple M., hired to sell the property wouldn't keep her informed as to progress regarding the sales. The broker, after many calls from Seta, finally returned a call to inform her that she (the broker) was directed by the chapter 11 trustee she was only to work with her, and we, the Mammolas, had no say regarding the property. Seta got in touch with her bankruptcy attorney, who was not her attorney, as of the appointment of the Chapter 11 trustee. At that point, she had been paid $110,000 to date from the S. R. M. Chapter 11 case. The attorney's response was he would talk to the trustee, which through no fault of his, went nowhere. Remember the conspiracy had a mind of its own (that being the chapter 7 trustee's plan).

I met the actual buyers on Labor Day 2010 at the rear of the property. I was called by one of the tenants who was locked out of his or her apartment. After letting the tenant in, as I was leaving, I picked up some newspapers and put them in the dumpster. Someone called out. I looked over at a group of people. One came over toward me and asked if I had anything to do with the building. I replied that I did. The woman said she was a realtor, and the people with her were very interested in buying the property. She had a listing sheet. She said they knew the price was $2,800,000. But they could only afford $2,600,000. The broker introduced me as the manager, as I told her I was. One of the gentlemen handed the broker a booklet of papers, which turned out to be his bank statements. They showed in excess of $1,000,000. The broker asked, "Is it possible for me to show them around?"

We walked around to the front. The minimarket was open, and we went in. The Ethiopian restaurant was open, so we walked through and into the rear common bathrooms, which were shared with the print shop next to the restaurant. Then we went to the foyer entrance to all seven apartments and the laundry area.

They had the broker make a verbal offer of $2,600,000 to buy as is. I said that the Mammola family would accept that offer. They were very happy, and we shook hands. The broker was to call Century 21 in the morning, and she did. About four weeks later, the chapter 11 trustee and the broker handled the sale. The price changed every other day, becoming less and less. The trustee and Seta fought over every reduction in price. The chapter 11 trustee said, "We don't have any other buyers, and I'm not going to lose this one."

Seta reminded her, "It was my husband who got these buyers." As for no other buyers, Seta reminded the chapter 11 trustee about the tenants who had deposits to buy their unit as a condo and that she was not honoring and not making an effort to pay them their deposits back.

The Chapter 11 trustee said, "We are not going through that again, regarding condos. I made it very clear that I have to sell this ASAP because of the Chapter 7 trustee. He is looking for $250,000 for your husband's chapter 7 case because of the bank's attorney telling him, behind closed doors, that R.J.M. was a 50 percent owner. And I'm not going to spend any of the trust money simply because I told you before if you fight him, the Chapter 7 trustee, the judge will automatically convert you to Chapter 7 liquidation."

It's very important here to point out we had no idea, nor did anyone bother to tell us that the court-appointed trustee, by federal law, had control *only* of the debtor's share (25 percent) of all three trusts, not complete control, as she belligerently did through this, as it turned out, *destruction* rather than reorganization of a very successful family real estate business of twenty-five years.

Seta again called her attorney. He said, "You're between a rock and a hard place."

She replied, "This just can't happen."

At this point in time, we did not know how wrong his statement was. Subsection 541 of the bankruptcy code states clearly that the trustee had control of the debtor's 25 percent. A simple hearing in front of the judge would clear up the ownership issue by having the attorney who made up the trust testify as to who the legal beneficiaries were, backed up by the registry of deeds' factual documentation. Seta said, "Because of a conspiracy scheme put into motion, all of you believe you're going to destroy our *family* and our business over greed for money. But I have told you a number of times, my husband won't let that be the case, believe me, once he understands what you people are really all about. I have been with him over twenty-three years. He is studying every motion filed in this case and his Chapter 7 case, copying every law that is referenced and how it applies. R.J.M. will know these laws as well as all of you. He has federal laws, the duties of a Chapter 7 and 11 trustee, and a copy of the US Constitution. When he is done, he will know them inside out. Then you, the Chapter 7 trustee and that judge will know who all of you are fighting or screwing around with, somebody who never learned how to lose a fight once he knows the rules. I'd usually say good luck. But I'm not a hypocrite. So my honest advice is hold on to your asses; Bobby is coming. You have said a number of times the Mammolas have a bigger fish to worry about—the Chapter 7 trustee. You can tell him and his puppet attorney their asses are already Bobby's. As for you, he knows every federal rule you have personally violated to date. The judge has openly, on record, in court stated just how biased she is against R.J.M. I don't know the rule or canon, regarding judges. You can be sure Bobby does or will when he is done putting all her actions on record. We wonder if she will regret letting her former partner, the chapter 7 trustee, run her courtroom. One thing I know, Chapter 11 reorganization, how you are handling—or should I say, *manipulating*—the sale of Triple M. by constantly reducing the sale price is headed to Chapter 11 destruction."

Seta, the trustee of Triple M., a week later, called the Chapter 11 trustee who had reduced the price from $2,600,000 to $1,900,000 just a week earlier, a loss of $700,000 of the attempted reorganization of a very successful family business and future income. She said, "I told you not to do it, but you did. The buyers check for $76,000 has bounced. At this point, I must insist that you cancel this sale. Then we can go back to the tenants who still have deposits on their units as condos. By law, those deposits preempt (interrupt or replace a scheduled program) your decision to make a quick package sale. The federal rule 1106 states, in part, the trustee is stepping into the debtor's shoes with an obligation of fairness to all parties in the case. These tenants with deposits, I have to believe they are parties of *interest* in the case, especially when you are holding their deposits on units that they still occupy and planned to buy. Let me be very clear; you, as the legal trustee and manager per Federal Rule 1106, are not walking in my shoes. We are the only ones following the Chapter 11 bankruptcy rules, as laid out at the 341 meeting and through the guidance of our attorney—I'm sorry, our former attorney before your appointment."

Needless to say, the bounced check was made good. Why would it not? They were at the price of $1,900,000. They knew they were paying less than half of the actual value and a lot less than they agreed to with R.J.M. They were buying now with a $76,000 deposit with the broker whom we hired. The broker was walking the buyers around in and out of the twelve stores, telling the tenants they were the new owners. As the tenants called me, the manager, and his assistant, Jerry, complaining about how rude the potential buyers were to them, it caused a ton of problems. First, the tenants with deposits, were looking for their money. Others wanted to know why they were not told the property had been sold. I assured them that my family were still the owners, which nobody believed, especially those who had deposits. I called the broker, asking, "What are you doing? We have not passed papers. Why did you do this?"

The broker's reply was "The trustee said it was OK." The broker went on to say, "You better do something about the crowed of people at the Bread of Life charitable organization tenant. The buyers want them gone."

I told the broker, "Try it again, but if you're smart, bring the police. Because nobody will bother our tenants again...and you can run back and tell that Chapter 11 and Chapter 7 trustee I'll be waiting. And she can bring the judge."

Jerry and I had a great relationship with the tenants for almost twenty years. Repairs were taken care of most of the time the same day or within a day or two. Jerry mostly convinced all the tenants that we were being fucked over by the court system. The tenants, after talking to Jerry, realized that was the case. In late November, the bank's attorney filed a motion in court for relief from the stay so they could foreclose on our property. The Chapter 7 trustee filed an objection motion with the court.

Remember, this trustee was the judge's former partner who was running the scheme in which he claimed I was a 50 percent owner of all the property, as I was told behind closed doors by the bank's attorney. The Chapter 11 trustee (this part is very important) filed a motion to stop the bank's motion for relief of stay, dated December 22, 2010). In essence, all the alleged facts that the bank was claiming against the debtor, such as not making all her payments, both mortgage and taxes, since her filing of Chapter 11 in May 2010 through December 2010 were incorrect. The court-appointed trustee (sua sponte) filed a motion, stating the debtor had made all payments from May 5, 2010, through December 22, 2010. That being the case, as stated by the court-appointed trustee, the debtor did everything right. We must remember all the motions filed in court. We were under the pains and penalties of perjury. Why was she appointed at all? (Oops, don't forget the Chapter 7 trustee's scheme or artifice of deception as to his greed for money, the $250,000 that he was fraudulently claiming.) The Chapter 7 trustee should see Federal Rule Section 157 (3), which states that a person who makes a false or fraudulent representation or claim will be fined or in prison for twenty years or both. One thousand one hundred and six crimes are set forth in 18 USC, subsection 152 (b). First of all, the bank's motion was only done in retaliation and spite to cost us money in court because of our refusal to cross-collateralize. A motion for the private sale of Triple M. in Malden, Massachusetts, was filed by the Chapter 11 trustee. The Chapter 7 trustee filed a motion to stop the sale after paying the bank's mortgage and the city taxes and liens just for Triple M. for the court to make an order to put the balance of the proceeds in escrow (approximately $400,000 according to the Chapter 11 trustee). This was just until the issue of me being a 50 percent owner of all the trust was resolved. The trick for the Chapter 7 trustee was huge. If I was not a 50 percent owner, the Chapter 7 trustee would lose his fraudulent criminal claim and deceptive scheme to steal $250,000 from Seta's Chapter 11 estate. We knew that the judge was not going to deny the Chapter 7 trustee, her former partner. So be it, it was an order. Let's remember in this artifice (a clever device to deceive) just who was running the courtroom (the one and only former partner, the chapter 7 trustee).

The definition of trustee is "an individual person or member of a board given control or powers of administration of property in trust with a legal obligation to administer it solely for the purpose, to be fair to all interested parties and the debtor."Uniform Trust Code, Chapter 11 Trustee Handbook. In the Seta's chapter 11 case, both the Chapter 7 and Chapter 11 trustee had no idea or, more truthfully, totally disregarded their legal *fiduciary* obligation. While all this court action was in play, the brilliant Chapter 11 trustee was still at work giving the buyers more money off the disaster price of $1,900,000. Seta R. Mammola, the trustee of Triple M., was still objecting to all the so-called business actions of the broker and the Chapter 11 trustee, regarding their continued calling of the tenants, trying to see who was staying, especially the charitable organization the Bread of Life. The buyers pushed hard for them to be gone before the closing. The Chapter 11 trustee paid the tenant in 11 Bickford Road, a single-family house, $3,500 to move out. (Remember the sale was "as is.") By this time, I have really dug into all the motions that had been filed in court by the Chapter 7 and 11 trustees and the banks through their attorneys. I am happy to say I was right on top of every violation of federal laws and the Civil Rights Act of 1983, which I documented and filed in court under the pains and penalties of perjury. Now the conspiracy scheme of artifice started to really show the total disregard for any attempt at justice. The bank's attorney (the one who told the Chapter 7 trustee that I was a 50 percent owner of all the trust) filed a motion on January 17, 2011, for the court to have an abundance of caution as to the Chapter 7 trustee's assertions and his position regarding my being a 50 percent owner in all of the trust property. The reason for this motion was the bank was done playing; they wanted to foreclose, and the Chapter 7 trustee was in their way. The Chapter 7 trustee fired back (pay attention here) with a motion of his own, which clearly stated it was the bank that told him that I was a 50 percent owner. (Here is where it gets interesting.) The Chapter 7 trustee had the moment that all people dream and pray for to shine (to perform as the best trustee or court officer) simply by doing his job, his fiduciary duty as required by the law he swore to uphold—that is report the bank and the bank's attorney for violating the law and a federal law at that (Fed section 157 (3), a scheme or artifice to defraud that person (the debtor's estate)). It says whoever knowingly (section 157 (3)) makes a false or fraudulent representation, claim, or promise concerning or in relation to a proceeding under title 11 at any time before or after the filing of the petition or in relation to a proceeding falsely asserted to be pending under such title shall be fined under this title, imprisoned not more than twenty years, or both. At that point, the Chapter 7 trustee violated the same federal law over greed of money. Remember while all of them are violating all these federal laws, I was documenting each and every violation. That would destroy all of them in a federal lawsuit by virtue as to the supreme law of the land, the Constitution of these United States of America. The judge had two motions on her bench. Only one could be the factual case. Classic con job, the judge disregarded both of them. Federal Rule, section 455 of title 28 governs the disqualification of federal judges, including bankruptcy judges, from acting in particular cases. Of relevance to this particular case are the requirements that a judge shall disqualify him- or herself in "any proceeding in which his impartiality might reasonably be questioned" or "where he has a personal bias or prejudice concerning a party" (28 USC subsection 455 (a) and (b) (1)). You think she stepped into it or what? Oh, remember back in October

Robert J. Mammola

29, 2010, the tyrant judge said, in open court, after she transferred my Chapter 7 into her court on October 25, 2010) that she always felt from the beginning that I was using my wife as a straw." The tyrant judge knew all this in four days. The Chapter 11 trustee filed in court a stipulation agreement that she forced the debtor and the three co-owners into under the threat that the judge would convert the Chapter 11 to a Chapter 7 if we tried to fight the Chapter 7 trustee. It was clear that the Chapter 7 trustee was going to get his fraudulent pound of flesh no matter how hard we fought; we agreed to pay the thief $100,000 so he would release his fraudulent hold on my Chapter 11 case. The bank made a motion to force the Chapter 11 trustee to honor the stipulation. In part, the stipulation by agreement with the co-owners was the trustee would use their share of Triple M. proceeds to pay Revere's taxes and liens. This agreement was a legal contract between the co-owners not debtors and the Chapter 11 trustee and became a court order. The trustee violated the agreement and the court order. The Chapter 11 trustee breached the contract by not paying Revere's taxes and liens. The Chapter 11 trustee violated a court order by not using the co-owners' proceeds as the contract specified. The Revere taxes and liens were accruing interest at 16 percent. The co-owners could have taken their share at the closing but chose to pay the Revere taxes and liens, which would have ended the Chapter 11 case in bankruptcy by removing the default in regard to the property in Revere, Massachusetts, on 10 and 14 Yeamans Street, a total of thirty-four units. The city of Revere filed a motion to make the Chapter 11 trustee abide by the court order approval of the stipulation contract with the co-owners. The bank filed motion after motion, regarding relief of stay of Ten Yeamans Realty Trust due to Revere's taxes and liens not being paid. (Remember, it was the bank that lied to the Chapter 7 Trustee as to me being a 50 percent owner of all three trusts.) Also keep in mind that each and every motion and their attorneys' billable time was paid out of my estate. I must jump back to the judge having two contradicting motions, one from the bank and the other from the Chapter 7 trustee. The Chapter 11 trustee never questioned either of them. By federal law, the Chapter 11 trustee had a fiduciary obligation. Federal rule 18 USC subsection 152 makes it a crime for any individual to "knowingly and fraudulently" make a false oath or a count in relation to a bankruptcy case, make a false proof of claim, or give, offer, receive, or attempt to obtain money. The Chapter 11 trustee had a fiduciary duty (Federal Rule 704) proof of claim.

Federal Rule 18 USC subsection 3057 requires a trustee to report suspected violations of federal criminal law to the appropriate US attorney. This federal law must be applied here so we can stay on top of the violations as they come up. Remember the bank's attorney walking around in superior court waving the phony beneficiary documents that never got filed at the registry of deeds and the attorney for the bank said that the bank didn't know who the real owners of the trusts were? Then, another attorney of the bank, after lying to the Chapter 7 trustee behind closed doors that I was a 50 percent owner in bankruptcy court in a motion filed, changed the bank's position, stating I was not the owner of record. The change in position from one court to another court is called judicial estoppel. Judicial estoppel is an inconsistent position of law applied to fact and pure law. You can't take a position in one court and change your position in another court, regarding the same matter. Meanwhile the Chapter 11 trustee and her personal law firm, who had a fiduciary obligation to protect the assets of the estate *did nothing*. The statutory duties of a Chapter 11 trustee are set forth in subsection 1106. Crimes are set forth in 18 USC Subsection 152 by any individual (as stated earlier). I filed a motion showing the inconsistencies that had been filed, but the judge thought it was a joke. She said the court would take no action (really). I just wanted the judge and her former partner to know I was still and would always be right there, just waiting for my turn at bat.

Now we are into the first week of February at the closing of the sale of Triple M. The closing took two days. The Chapter 11 trustee gave in concessions to the buy for $19,500. Remember this sale was an as-is sale that started out at $2,600,000 and ended up under $1,900,000. How could she just keep giving the estate's money away when she had a fiduciary obligation to the debtor to protect the assets of the debtor's estates by law? Another thing the Chapter 11 trustee did not want to talk about or give any thought to was the $80,000 in credit cards that were owed. I made it very clear to her I called each of them and told them our best property was to be sold as condos and everyone would be paid in full from the sale. The Chapter 11 trustee said, "Don't count on that happening." Seta, the debtor, and Diane, the new property manager, stated in the 341 meeting that the $80,000 in credit cards would be paid from the sale of Triple M. as condos. Later you will see how the US trustee addressed the chapter 11 trustee's attitude regarding the credit cards among other issues. Now Triple M. was sold. The trustee had put approximately $400,000 into an escrow account according to her court order. The gas and electric bills were not paid (it was sold February 11, 2011 and still owed July 1, 2014. Tenants with deposits were still not paid (about $23,000) as of July 1, 2014. The tenant at 525 Main Street owed $14,500 in back rent. The Chapter 11 trustee was involved with the Chapter 7 trustee's scheme to steal $250,000 from my Chapter 11 case. She would not chase the back rent and wouldn't allow us to hire an attorney to the start eviction process. We were in March 2011. The bank had filed another motion for relief from stay because of the revere taxes and liens not paid per contract of co-owners. Again, in March, the bank filed an emergency motion to hold off on the motion of relief of stay. (What stinks here?) Either the bank wanted relief or they didn't. What really happened was if the judge gave the relief of stay, then the judge's former partner's scheme or artifice regarding my 50 percent ownership would be out the window. Chapter 7 would have no payday.

"This is good," we were being told. They said that the agreement to pay off the Chapter 7 thief has to be signed. It was strange; Triple M. had been sold, but only the four girls had to sign at the closing. One would think if I owned 50 percent of the property, I would have had to sign the closing documents. Seta, the debtor, put a motion to the court that questioned that fact, which was totally ignored by the judge. The City of Revere put in a motion for the trustee to pay the taxes, per the trustee's motion for a private sale of Triple M. and the contract with the co-owners to use their share as agreed. With all this court action going on, the Chapter 7 and 11 trustees put in a motion to have the agreement signed and become a court order. How many federal laws were broken in this batch of motions? How many billable hours were being billed to the Seta's estate just so they could consummate this barrel of lies and deception? The real problem we had now was the massive amount of what the trustees, the attorneys, and the banks were billing under the codename "administrative costs," plus the accumulated interest and penalties in regard to the taxes and liens not being paid and openly executed or simply just violated. Does anyone question who was running the Chapter 11 destruction?

the Chapter 7 trustee? (Why would anyone call a thief trustee?)

the Chapter 7 trustee? (He is the only one not working but being paid $100,000 based on a motion of lies and deception.)

with absolute approval from the judge, like old times, her former partner.

Diane and Michela, trust co-owners filed an affidavit in the bankruptcy court. They both were so heartbroken as to what a disaster our lives had become. How out of control the Chapter 11 trustee was! They hand-wrote the affidavit at 2:00 a.m. and filed it at 9:00 a.m. the next morning before court. The judge asked who they were. (Remember this judge approved Diane to be the new property manager of all the trusts.) Diane stood up and said, "I am the property manager, Your Honor."

The judge, as rudely as she could, said, "This motion has ten violations and is not accepted," waving the affidavit. The judge must have forgottenCanon 3A(5) "In disposing of matters promptly, efficiently, and fairly, a judge must demonstrate due regard for the rights of the parties to be heard and have issues resolved without unnecessary cost or delay..." www.uscourts.gov (I must ask the reader to reflect back to the substantive doctrine, which was clearly explained in detail earlier.) In addition, if the judge was so cognizant as to procedures being adhered to, why did she allow the Chapter 11 trustee not to follow the Federal Rule of procedures 11 U.S.C. § 704 as to proof of a claim—that being the Chapter 7 trustee's fraudulent claim that I was a 50 percent owner of all three trusts without any factual evidence. Seta filed an affidavit that would bring most people to tears—not the tyrant. The truth be known, she loved the hurt she allowed to be done in her court of *injustices*. Remember the scheme or artifice to sabotage my family now had a mind of its own.

I have not mentioned this purposely. My wife and I are living apart. With all my family had been put through, not being with her is too much. I am the type of guy who loves his wife and family and would rather not live without her or my family. It has been over four years that we have been apart and all over this turmoil. Our lives have turned into a living hell all because we got caught up in something we had no control over—turning the property into condos at a time when the real estate market was collapsing. Our bank really was a good bank. I had a great relationship with them. The vice president who handled my family's accounts was and still is a great guy. (Remember when that excuse of a counsel visited all the property early on our return trip back at the Malden parking lot, the vice president apologized and said it was out of his control. The bank got caught with their pants down by the FDIC unbeknown to any of the bank's customers. Certainly we didn't know. Had I known the bank had a problem with the F.DIC, I would not have taken over 10 Milano Avenue, which the CEO of the bank asked me to do. It saved the bank over $90,000, as stated in the minutes of the bank's board of directors meeting. Also, just to be clear, the CEO of the bank knew, my taking over of 10 Milano Avenue would be removing a problem loan for the *bank*. I had a HUD loan in place to refinance all the family property at a lower interest rate. The CEO said, "No. Stay with us, and we will make all the loans 5 percent, across the board. All the loans at 5 percent interest would have saved in monthly payments $5,200 per month.

Refinancing with our bank seemed to be a win-win. But it was not and could not have taken place. Sad to say, the CEO of the bank knew just how deceptive his promise to me, regarding the refinancing of all our loans. It was due to the cease and desist order of the FDIC.

Today is not a good day. As a matter of fact, it's a fucking terrible day. The attorney the Chapter 11 trustee replaced after being appointed trustee just called and said he needed to file a final bankruptcy plan, which the debtor has to sign. This attorney is a really good person. Making this call is the last thing he wanted to do, but the Chapter 11 trustee—that piece of work—called him for help in communicating with the debtor and her family. In spite of all the heartache, pain, suffering, separation, and financial disaster we have endured, we are still a family. My—no *our* response was to tell her the suit against her and her law firm for breach of fiduciary obligation to the debtor and the breach of the contract she made with the co-owners is in the millions. Also a $100,000,000 dollar suit was filed against the tyrant judge, the Chapter 7 trustee, his attorney, his law firm, the bank's attorneys, and their law firm. I guess now would be a good time to let all of you know that the district attorney's office and the attorney general's office has been extremely helpful—or should I say, informative after going over the numerous federal laws that the group as a whole have blatantly violated without any thought of *justice*. I know this is a strange word. The attorney generals and the district attorney's assistants gave us the proper venue as to where complaints about our Constitutional rights being denied must be filed—that being the federal district court. It was made very clear to us that the political abuse or BS had no place in federal court. The case did not belong in superior court, as our attorney mistakenly filed our original suit. But trust me, we would do whatever it took legally to ram the meaning of that word (hold on) *justice* down each one of their throats. Now I can get back to the pleasure of working on saving our Constitutional rights by pursuing a jury trial by right, which our forebears, many of whom gave their lives for our future as a free country, guaranteed by the US Constitution. Certainly, the framers of the Constitution did not fight for our freedom just to allow the government, which was formed by the new states, to take it. So the states could stand together and form a more perfect union, because as a united union, the new states would be much stronger together, and they could defend their new freedom. The Constitution was made in the form of a contract between the states, which gave the new government specific powers. Those powers are clear, which prevents even the possibility of any chance of a dictator (a ruler with total power) and any acts of tyranny (cruel, unreasonable, or arbitrary use of power or control). Thomas Jefferson said, "Experience hath shown, that even under the best forms of government those entrusted with power have, in time and by slow operations perverted it into Tyranny."

The sad thing is nobody can give my family the past four years back or wipe out all the memories and heartache we as family have been put through. How true Jefferson's statement. Keep in mind the judge took an oath to serve, protect, and defend the Constitution of the United States of America, "so help me God." It is the supreme law of the land. This judge allowed two motions to cross her bench of justice without even a thought of questioning which of the two were factual. This goes way beyond the question of tyranny. We the people must stand up and at whatever the price claim back the freedom our forebears fought for with their lives and hammered out in the US Constitution's seven articles and twenty-seven amendments, the first ten of which are the Bill of Rights. These enumerate every citizen's rights. Alexander Hamilton said, "If the federal government should overpass the just bounds of its Authority and make a Tyrannical use of its Powers, the people, whose creature it is, must appeal to the standard they have formed, and take such measures to redress the injury done to the Constitution as the exigency may suggest and prudence justify" (December 26, 1787). The framers of the Constitution knew that government tended toward tyranny. That's why the language is unambiguous and unmistakable in the Bill of Rights and the entire contract. The US Constitution clearly states as a contract that every citizen of the United States is endowed by their creator ("God Almighty") with certain inalienable rights (life, liberty, and the pursuit of happiness), which the government, by virtue of the powers of the Constitution, is bound to secure. The judge, when she took her oath of affirmation, must have missed or forgotten Article 3, which states judges may stay in office under good behavior; Article 6.2, which states judges in every state will be bound by the US Constitution, the supreme law of the land; and Amendment 14, which says no state may make or enforce any law that diminishes the privileges or freedoms of citizens of the United States.

No state may take away any person's life, liberty, or property without proper operation of the law. No state may deny any person under its authority the equal protection of the laws (or due diligence). The judge showed total disregard for all of these when she so rudely stated in open court she would not give any consideration to the evidence or argument as to the facts laid out in Diane and Michela's affidavit (the evidence she would not accept). It has now been about four months since the sale of the Triple M. property. The balance of the money is still in escrow. The number of motions and billable hours from all the attorneys and the amount of court costs are insurmountable. If we don't find money, we lose everything. At this point, the judge has allowed Triple M. to be sold for less than half its market value. In March 2011, the judge gave the bank relief of stay on the 14 Yeamans Street realty trust, a three-condo property. The co-owners proceeds were put into escrow instead of paying Revere's taxes and liens as was laid out at the 341 meeting with the US trustee. Remember the judge put Triple M. proceeds into escrow until determination in court as to the true owners of all three trust properties, which never took place. The judge kept postponing a hearing regarding ownership issues. We can't forget that Revere's taxes and liens are accruing at 16 percent. The city filed motion after motion for the judge to have the Chapter 11 trustee, as per the agreement the trustee made with the co-owners to pay Revere out of the Triple M. sale. Now the trustee has destroyed this Chapter 11 reorganization plan by following the Chapter 7 trustee's scheme or artifice. The US trustee has made a motion in court to clarify the Chapter 11 trustee's failure to provide adequate information regarding the proposed plan of reorganization, the disclosure statement and plan's amendment to consistently state what the class 5 creditors were going receive, and C) the trustee's proposed settlement to the Chapter 7 trustee. If accepted, he will be paid upon confirmation of the plan. (Now the truth is peeking out.) With the US trustee, these questions would never be asked. The US trustee's only mission would be to honor and to serve justice. This is the same US trustee who held the 341 meeting with Seta and Diane, at which time, this trustee approved the debtor's reorganization plan to sell Triple M. as condos. And on record, the debtor would pay the mortgage and the taxes on both Malden and Revere. She would also pay 100 percent of the credit card debt and have a profit of over $2,000,000 when the condo project was completely sold out.

The US trustee congratulated both the debtor, Seta, and Diane, the newly appointed manager; gave both of them a hug; and said they were very lucky girls and would be out of bankruptcy in a short period of time. We have this on audio and transcribed also. As stated earlier, Diane, for the first six months, did all the monthly operating reports as to rents, mortgage, taxes, utility, and maintenance—a total reconciliation of all the rents that came in and the payments that went out. Out of nowhere, the tyrant appointed a trustee without any just cause. This is where the judge overstepped her bounds. The framers of the Constitution labeled this act *usurpation*, which is taking the place of someone in a position of power illegally, contrary to or forbidden by law. I filed a motion for clarification of declaratory relief, which laid out the federal laws that had been violated. What do you think the judge did? You're right. She threw it out. I knew she would. At this point, I knew exactly how she would respond. Even though the law calls for the court to resolve any issues of law before a case can go on or a jury trial by right. Here is her order.

> Full docket text for document 102; Order dated July 1st 2011 99 motion filed by debtor Robert J. Mammola for Clarification and Declaratory Relief counts, as well as Affidavit; it's attached re: 93 affidavit of Robert J. Mammola. Motion denied for the reasons set forth in the Chapter 7 trustee's opposition. Moreover, the relief requested, to the extent Movant requests a declaratory judgment, procedurally improper.

The judge's total disregard for priority action over court scheduling (USC § 1062.3) prevented justice when a declaration of right of fact trial by jury is a right. Again the tyrant belligerently ignored the supreme law of the land, the US Constitution. Right here the conspiracy (a secret plan by a group to do something unlawful or harmful) is jumping off the page. This is tyranny at its boldest and most arrogant (absolute abuse of power).

J.Feeney denied, RJM'S MOTION OF DECLARATORY CLARIFICATION [This is a total different case in 2009 where Justice Scalia stressed that both factors must be satisfied.] Id. at 1760-61 (2009) (citations omitted). The Court then observed that, in determining whether the movant has met its burden, the "legal principles have been distilled into consideration of four factors": "(1) whether the stay applicant has made a strong showing that he is likely to succeed on the merits; (2) whether the applicant will be irreparably injured absent a stay; (3) whether issuance of the stay will substantially injure the other parties interested in the proceeding; and (4) where the public interest lies." Id. at 1761 (citing Hilton v. Braunskill, 481 U.S. 770, 776 (1987)). See also Philidor v. U. S. Att'y Gen., 384 Fed. Appx. 876, 878 (11th Cir. 2010).3 Of these four factors, the first two "are the most critical." Nken, 129 S. Ct. at 1761. Indeed, in his concurring opinion in Nken (joined in by Justice Scalia), Justice Kennedy stressed that both factors must be satisfied,

The judge in pursuit of justice not only had no interest in the declaratory relief motion. The judge had absolutely no interest in my affidavit. Really, how could she? Both the declaratory motion for relief and the affidavit plainly laid out the Constitutional and Federal Rules that were violated. My wife and daughter made another affidavit.

> Honorable Judge, January 3, 2011, my daughter and I would like you to please take a moment to see our position and needs in regard to our Chapter 11 plan to reorganize. The decision to sell our family home was a very

difficult decision for all of us to make. After the disaster the Chapter 11 trustee made with the sale of Triple M., we had no other choice but sell our home in order to keep our Revere income property so we did. I am proud to say our mortgages were always paid, which were automatically withdrawn by the bank every month. As a matter a fact, the Mammolas were considered one of the Boston bank's best customers, until they were issued a cease and desist order from the FDIC. At which time the bank tried to force us to cross-collateralize all of our mortgages, and when we declined is when this retaliation, deceptive and unfortunate situation began. By making the Mammolas cross-collateralize, it would strengthen the bank's position with FDIC order to cease and desist. In addition, at the 341 meeting, which Diane and I attended, it was very clear the plan would be that through the sale of Triple M. Property in Malden, MA, all the taxes and liens would be paid for both Revere and Malden and the Chapter 11 bankruptcy would be over.

The affidavit goes on. The judge gave this hearty cry for help and more important a cry for justice zero—and we mean *zero*—consideration. That's what the judge calls justice. I call it tyranny (a cruel and oppressive government). My wife and daughter hired a realtor we have dealt with for over twenty-five years. Seta, as trustee of our home at 34 Mammola Way in Medford, Massachusetts, signed an agreement to put the property on the market for $850,000. When the Chapter 11 trustee got involved with the realtor, they tried to lower the price. Seta called the chapter 11 trustee and the broker. She told them both, "Don't even try to come into our home with a buyer with a sale price starting less than $850,000." The less-than-honest broker had a buyer at a lower asking price. As a matter of fact, the less-than-honest brokers had two parties who put bids on our home—one for $700,000 and another for $720,000. The Chapter 11 trustee told the broker to accept whichever one could perform quickly. The broker, an old friend of ours, accepted the $720,000 offer. Remember Seta, the debtor, signed a contract with this broker to list the house for $850,000. One of the buyers showed up with a builder. I told them to get the fuck off the property and to tell the broker and that piece of shit trustee just to try to make us sell our home at that price. "Get ready for a fucking war." I also told them to tell that judge just to try to force this issue. I was ready and had had enough of her and her weasel former partner. I'd be waiting.

Our home sold for $780,000. My whole life, those who bothered me or my family, I would tell them once that I did not want any trouble but only once. I knew that excuse for a man (the consultant for the bank) needed a good, old-fashioned East Cambridge serious beating. "No," I said, "I'm not a kid. I'm a gentleman, no matter what my street smarts might want, and I truly believe in the law and in justice." I had no idea that a judge could be a tyrant and could ignore and have total disregard for the law. This judge took an oath to support and defend the supreme law of the land, the Constitution of these United States of America. My luck, I got this Chapter 7 thief for a trustee. He had total control of his former partner's courtroom (the tyrant judge). True, the bank misled him, but being a thief, once he knew the bank out and out lied, it was too late. The greed in the thief was more important than the truth. He swore and took a solemn oath to pursue justice. The judge, both the Chapter 7 and Chapter 11 trustees, their attorneys, and the bank don't even know how to spell *justice*. I am taking an oath and making a promise to spend the rest of my life making all of them pay for what they put my family through so help me God. When the bank lied to the thief, the Chapter 7 trustee, that was the beginning of the sabotage, scheme, artifice, and destruction of the Mammola empire to quote the thief as stated in his motion filed in the tyrant's court with uncontrollable drool (saliva) flowing from his greedy mouth.

Back to the sale of our home at 34 Mammola Way in Medford, Massachusetts—as for that Chapter 11 trustee, Bob Mammola is far from done with her. She never came back to our home, but she wasn't done giving our money away. The less-than-honest brokers had a radon test and a mold test. My daughter Diane had problems with her health. She asked the broker, regarding the test for radon and mold, if there would be any gases or fumes. If so, she planned to stay at her sister's house. The brokers and both companies guaranteed her that there would be none. They lied, Diane had severe reactions, ending up in the emergency room due to both for both. The radon test emitted gases to detect it, and the mold test let out spores, which made her sick for almost a month. You must know by now that the trustee and the less-than-honest brokers could have cared less about Diane's health problems. Her medical records will show which medications and how long she was on them and how much discomfort she was put through from those. I'm sorry that we, to be safe, just had Diane stay at her sister's house. The radon test was OK. The mold test, they claimed, was very bad. We knew this was BS. Diane would not have been able to live in the house. I borrowed five hundred dollars from my brother Paul to have a mold test done. We did have Diane stay with her sister for a week. The mold test took two weeks to come back. The results were negative. The brokers and trustees test results were known the day after the tests were done. Strangely, with our test, it took two weeks for the results to come back. The trustee had no interest in our test. She had the judge reduce the price of the house by $15,000 because of mold.

    The buyers seemed like nice people. The day before the closing, they had a walk through with the listing broker's husband. They were very nice; they heard I smoked cigars and brought me one. We all walked around so they could check the house out. While downstairs, I showed the buyers the wall where the inspector claimed the mold was. On either side of the fireplace, there was a sliding panel for access, which the inspector did not know about. The buyer looked in and saw that the wall was completely dry, with no sign of mold. He turned to me and said, "We will credit the money back." Then we went into the utility room, and the broker took a picture of the oil tank so they could calculate what the buyers owed to the sellers for the oil. Somehow, that bill for the oil did not get paid at the closing. The broker and the trustee would not pursue the payment. Finally, we took the buyers to district court.

The magistrate said it should have been paid at the closing. I explained that the trustee handled the passing because of the bankruptcy. The magistrate replied, "That's what it is." So another $965 was thrown away. So much for the buyers being nice people. Remember the house was to be sold to pay administrative bills—another way of referring to court costs, attorneys' bills, and the Chapter 11 trustee's ever-increasing bill. But being the deceitful, unworthy trustee that she is, during the process of selling our home so we could keep our last piece of income property, the gem of an unworthy trustee filed a motion to abandon that property behind our backs. The fact is we were the only ones who didn't know. My daughter Diane and I compiled a list of questions regarding the disaster the Chapter 11 reorganization turned out to be. We made a list of Constitution articles and amendments that were violated, along with each and every federal rule or law. Diane and I put all these facts together so a motion could be filed to remove the Chapter 11 trustee and presented it to the court. The factual documentation we compiled included the violations of the law. We would turn this whole conspiracy scheme they thought they were getting away with upside down to stick it right in that tyrant's face. We would show her and her former partner just how ignorant they both were to wake up a sleeping streetfighter. Take my word, neither of those deceitful saboteurs are a match for Diane and me. We called for this meeting. When we arrived, we were happy to see all our attorneys present—my attorney, who recommended Seta's bankruptcy attorneys, and my daughter Michela's attorney. Remember we brought all this important documentation we compiled, but to our surprise, somehow they turned it around. They thought they were going to break the bad news to us. Even with our home being sold, there was not enough money to pay all the administrative bills (legal bills).

I said very calmly, "What's going on here? We wanted this meeting to go over all the violations."

They said, "Sorry, we have bigger problems."

Where did we hear that before? I looked around the table, at each and every one of them. My precious daughter Diane had tears in her eyes

And asked" where were we supposed to live in our cars, and they all just shrugged"!. I said, "Honey, please don't cry in front of these MFs, not over money. Come, please. We're out of here. I looked at my old attorney. He just put his hand up.

Michela's attorney said, "This is it. Nothing can be done."

and I got up. I said, "Fuck all of you," especially to my old attorney. Michela's attorney went to say something stupid. I said, "Shut up. You're fired. You were hired to protect Michela's half of the proceeds from the sale of her home, which was to be left in the Chapter 11 reorganization plan, so as to save 10 Yeamans Realty, the family's last piece of income property. Instead, you were handled by that excuse of a trustee and tried to convince your client, Michela, to go along with the Chapter 11 trustee. Just to be clear, all of what I have said to you is in e-mail. And for the rest of you, Michela will be taking her share of 34 Mammola Way. If you were short for administrative bills before now, you're short another $400,000. Ready, Di? We don't need this bullshit."

The debtor's attorney went to say something, but Michela's attorney, who had just been terminated for working with the Chapter 11 trustee's plan, said, "Bob, we can give Michela $3,500."

Money was tight. It's funny; that was what the Chapter 11 trustee had been saying all along. The Boston bank's attorney said the bank did not believe there was $375,000 profit in the 34 Mammola Way property. That was the reason they gave for filing a motion to foreclose on 10 Yeamans realty and not living up to the agreement. With 34 Mammola Way sold to pay the Revere taxes and liens, the bank would leave the mortgage on 10 Yeamans as it was. As it turns out, they were right. There was over $500,000 profit in 34 Mammola Way. Michela hired an attorney, which was the advice of the judge. The former Chapter 11 attorney, before the sabotage scheme, was put into play. And the tyrant judge illegally appointed the trustee. Michela's attorney was to make sure her share was being left in the chapter 11 bankruptcy case. We would keep our last piece of income property. In a number of e-mails, it was clear that her attorney was being controlled by the Chapter 11 trustee. Michela was not getting what she hired him for, that being a written guarantee as to us keeping 10 Yeamans Street property. Michela had no choice but to terminate him, which she did. Again, the sabotage scheme was still in play. Remember it had a mind of its own. Now anyone who could grab a piece of the Mammolas estate did. The judge did give the bank relief of stay, which we can't forget. The judge was to have a hearing regarding true ownership. That never took place (so no facts and no justice).

We did not know at that time about Massachusetts law on the right of survivorship and rights of possession. Neither did our own attorneys, or they just did not enforce it on their clients' behalf, which precludes any administrative cost taken from a family residence.

What did take place was a hearing regarding her former partner's fraudulent claim of $250,000, which had changed to $100,000. A hearing date (May 5, 2011) was entered on February 24, 2012. The judge claimed, after studying the agreement, her position was filed. Here it is exactly, per court documentation recorded.

> The Court: All right. Does anyone wish to be heard on the motion to approve the stipulation between the two estates?
> Attorney for the Chapter 7 Trustee: The recitation substantially comports with the motion, Your Honor. We have no objection.
> The Court: All right. No objection has been filed, and there's been no request for an opportunity to be heard today at the hearing. I have reviewed the terms of the compromise and find that they are fair and reasonable and are in the best interests of both estates and approve the compromise and grant the motion in both cases.

The judge unjustly, claimed no objection had been filed. She must have forgotten my motion. The judge knew she was speaking less than the truth. I had filed a sixty-page motion on December 28, 2010, which, through certified documentation, proved the Chapter 7 trustee, his attorney, and his law firm, with their overwhelming motion of evidence that I was a 50 percent owner of all the trusts were totally fabricating the facts—in plain English, it was a barrel of lies. My motion was filed December 28, 2010, docket 215, and the judge refused to hear the motion regarding the Chapter 7 scheme and artifice, a trick to deceive others. Just to be clear, I did object to that illegal claim and was denied the chance to prove the Chapter 7 trustee was misleading the court of justice. As to any objection or anyone who wanted to be heard—surprise! We were not in court that day. The Chapter 11 trustee guaranteed the judge would convert the Chapter 11 to a Chapter 7 liquidation if I opposed. Also at that hearing, the hold on the money from the Triple M. sale was vacated. At that point in time, the Chapter 11 trustee had no excuse not to live up to her obligation in the contract with the co-owners to pay the Revere taxes and liens as agreed. And she was under a court order by that contract, but she just violated it. At that same hearing, the city of Revere made a motion for the trustee to perform as to the agreement with the co-owners. Again, the trustee did what she wanted and held on to the money. The judge froze the proceeds from Triple M. until the owner issue was resolved, which never took place. It was just continuance or postponement after postponement, and so on without any legal resolution. What did take place at that May 5, 2010) was documented in the court records. The judge, the Chapter 11 trustee, and the attorney for the City of Revere all violated the court order of January 19, 2011, which stated that from the Triple M. sale, the Revere taxes and liens would be paid. At that same hearing, the contract between the co-owners and the Chapter 11 trustee was totally illegally breached. A new plan, contrary or opposed to the desires was agreed upon in the contract form made with the co-owners' proceeds. This new plan stopped the Revere taxes and liens from being totally paid off and continued the 16 percent interest to the detriment of the estate and to the detriment of the co-owners' proceeds not being used according to the contract they made with the trustee. They did not pay the Revere taxes and liens as specified in the contract. The default still exists with the bank. The Chapter 11 case continues, and the legal cost continues to grow. The Mammola family once had a very successful real estate business, but as planned by the Chapter 7 trustee's scheme or artifice, which now had its own agenda, it was now totally decimated. Remember, all these motions and court costs were charged to the estate of Seta R. Mammola, the debtor, without any questions from the judge. Article 1.10 of the Constitution of the United States is very Clear: no state may pass any law that interferes with private contracts or grant any title of nobility. The tyrant must have forgotten her oath: "I do solemnly swear or affirm that I will support and defend the Constitution of the United States against all enemies, foreign and domestic; that I take this obligation freely, without any mental reservation or purpose of evasion. So help me God." To the reader, it's important to repeat the violation. The purpose of the Constitution is to bind power and unleash liberty.

Now the case and the court action continued with total disregard for the co-owners' binding contract or any form of justice. Back to the sale of Mammola Way, our home for the past twenty-four years—It was sold so we could keep our last piece of income property in Revere, Massachusetts. Now, after being told if we sold our home, it would let us keep the Revere property, at the meeting my daughter and I thought we called, our attorneys were telling us that the total administrative bills were too much and Michela wouldn't have tuition to finish her last year at Suffolk University, at which she was on the dean's list. How this happened, I don't know. The agreement was if Michela put her share of the Mammola Way sale into the chapter 11 plan, she would keep $50,000 for moving out of our home and pay Suffolk University. Her share of the house plus the balance of the Triple M. sale would fund the Chapter 11 plan. Now that the house was being sold with her share, it was not enough. That was BS. The trustee for the Chapter 11 had yet another trick. The mortgage on Mammola Way was flawed. The bank did not record it properly. We had been paying it for the last six years. Through some bankruptcy rule, called the "strong arm," the trustee did not have to pay the mortgage. Now if the mortgage was not legal, then we didn't owe it. The trustee suddenly was claiming half of the

$300,000. Because the mortgage was not owed, the administrative bills instantly grew overnight. (How?) The plan was based on Mammola Way being sold at $700,000 with the Mammola family keeping the 10 Yeamans Street Realty Trust property in Revere, Massachusetts. The actual sale price was $780,000. The bankruptcy rules were that each bill had to be defined and a broken down and shown to the court and the debtor. Never happened with the tyrant. We had no say. Seta owned half the house. The trustee (what a joke calling her or the Chapter 7 trustee someone you *trust*) got to claim it, but only to the extent that the money was needed for the estates. Legitimate bills. Keep in mind this is what's called a windfall. The closing was calculated with this money being paid to the bank so as to pay off the mortgage. Remember, this scheme or artifice has a mind of its own. But it's not a problem. The judge would not question the Chapter 11 trustee. Ready for this, the greedy Chapter 11 trustee wanted all the back payments that we made. This court action had been going on over one year. The motion the Chapter 11 trustee filed in court was three part: the mortgage was not owed to the bank, all the payments made from the time Seta filed for Chapter 11 reorganization (another big joke) the trustee wanted back (more than $23,000), and most importunately, the trustee wanted all payments for the five years prior (more than $100,000). The judge declared the mortgage was not valid or not owed. That was count A. In counts B and C, the judge wanted the Chapter 11 trustee to provide more proof regarding all the payments that were made.

    I must at this point reflect back to the fraudulent claim of the Chapter 7 trustee. Why didn't the judge require him to supply proof of his fraudulent claim as to my 50 percent ownership of all three trust properties. The trustee, by law, was to pay Michela half that mortgage money. The trustee ignored Michela's request. Michela filed an emergency motion to the court to be paid her half of the money, which was hers, being half owner, for more college funds and for an investment property. (Remember the Federal Rule—no administrative cost were to be taken out of a residential property of the debtor, spouse, or co-owner.) The trustee filed a motion for the court to allow her to pay Michela on the next court date, which was in two months. The Trustee stated that the emergency, if there was any, was not of her doing. The trustee also stated in her motion that Michela had just bought a four-family piece of property in Malden. Michela was not in bankruptcy, and the Chapter 11 trustee had no legal reason to know Michela's business (or hold her money). The judge replied, "No, we will hear this emergency motion in November," which was ninety days away (a month longer). The Chapter 11 trustee, after seventy days, made an agreement with Michela's attorney to give her $110,000 and hold $40,000 until counts B and C were settled. It's now eighteen months later. The trustee and the bank have settled for Seta's estate and Michela's to receive half of the $10,385 settlement, half for each of the owners. The Chapter 11 trustee now owes Michela $45,187.50. The Chapter 11 trustee is now saying she will pay Michela after she figures out the cost of this court action, half of which will be billed to Michela. The windfall is $150,000, which the judge is allowing her to steal (for what, why, or whom?) and then pass half the cost onto Michela. (This will be a great question to a jury in our lawsuit.) Remember this trustee wouldn't spend any of the trust money to fight the Chapter 7 trustee, regarding his fraudulent scheme or artifice (a clever or cunning device used to trick or deceive others.) Also the mortgage money was a windfall, which the judge is allowing her (the trustee) to keep no questions asked. An important point, the Mammolas are learning the federal rules as the scheme or artifice is being played out. More clearly put, had the co-owners known in January of 2011; they, as co-owners, could have taken their share of the sale of Triple M. and paid off Revere's taxes and liens themselves. They would have. The co-owners also would have known enough and had the money to hire an attorney to have the court make the Chapter 7 trustee, by a jury trial, prove his fraudulent proof of claim. The Chapter 11 trustee's duties are set forth in Federal Rule Subsection 1106 and S.S. 704 (5) (proof of claim, which incorporates by reference certain Chapter 7 trustee duties as specified in Subsection (704), as stated in section 5 (if a purpose would be served, examine proofs of claims and object to the allowance of any claim that is improper). Remember the judge had the proceeds put into Escrow until true ownership was determined. All that BS regarding a hearing that never took place, I know someone could say, "The co-owners didn't have the money, how could they hire an attorney?" But with $400,000 in escrow, by the tyrant's court order, hiring the best attorneys in Boston would not have been a problem. Think of all the court costs, attorney fees, and the 16 percent accruing penalty and interest. The new attorney would have stopped that. We know this now. With the utmost disheartening reality, with all the attorneys being paid or involved in some way or another in Seta's chapter 11 case, none of them just stepped up and said to us, "Just do this. Have the co-owners take their share of the Triple M. sale." Please be assured the Mammola family has been robbed by all the injustice that has been allowed by a judge who took an oath to pursue justice. To go back to the sale of 34 Mammola Way, the Chapter 11 trustee in Seta's case, by federal law, was bound to protect and preserve the assets of the estate (S.S. 345). The trustee put in the purchase and sale that we would be charged $240 a day if not out on the closing date. The judge approved that purchase and sale with that clause. This $240-a-day fine is just payback from the Chapter 11 trustee not being allowed by the insistence of the debtor, Seta, to give our home a way for $720,000. The trustee gave the buyers $15,000 for mold that did not exist. (The court order approving the sale stated "as is and where is.") The trustee would not work with Michela's new attorney at the closing. That cost us another $950. The trustee intentionally did not collect the oil refund owed to us. It was almost May 2013, three years in bankruptcy. The Chapter 7 trustee's greedy, sneaky, deceitful, cowardly conspiracy plan to sabotage the Mammola family has worked. The judge finally gave relief of stay to the bank to foreclose on 10 Yeaman's Realty in Revere, Massachusetts.

She stated I was not the owner of record without a hearing only after the tyrant gave the Chapter 11 trustee permission to abandon the property, allowing her not to pay any of the city of Revere's taxes and liens per her court order. Influence is the power to have an important effect on someone or something. If someone influences someone else, he or she is changing a person or thing. To the reader, I have been looking for the right time or place to infuse this unbelievable, superfantastic *violation* allowed by the judge, who was entrusted to make sure all sides are holding to the rules of *justice*. She claimed that my motion for declaratory relief and Diane's and Michela's handwritten motion were procedurally wrong, when, in fact, they were not wrongly filed by definition of the Fourteenth Amendment of the Constitution. Massachusetts law was laid out. (The most difficult issues are likely to arise in cases involving valuable residential property inhabited by the co-owner. Since these properties ordinarily are single-family homes, the potential for renting a portion of the property to another party is usually nonexistent. Any question will ultimately turn on the particular state property law that is applicable. Massachusetts law held that nothing in Section 363 (h) would destroy the nondebtor wife's survivorship interest if a sale were authorized, and therefore, a sale was impractical because the trustee would be required to hold the proceeds until the debtor received her full interest, either upon her death or divorce. However, the court then went on to state, citing Coombs, in re: Ray. n45 and other cases, that deciding the detriment to the nondebtor spouse to be measured under the third section 363 (h) requirement would include valuing her survivorship interest as well as her present possessory interest n46 (nondebtor's right of possession and survivorship in her lifetime).

Another case *In re Persky* quoted a Supreme Court opinion, which in another context, stated, "We are not blind to the fact that in practical terms financial compensation may not always be a completely adequate substitute for a roof over one's head" (n50). This explanation may suggest that the factors other than monetary benefit or detriment are to be considered only as additional reasons why the property should not be sold and not as reason that could overcome the results of the basic financial analysis. The court in *In re Coombs* further justified its refusal to order a sale by noting that a sale and consequent move would cause the nondebtor spouse "psychological stress that would operate upon a deteriorating mental condition" and physical difficulties inherent in adapting to new surroundings suitable for one who depends upon a wheelchair. Where has the money from our home and the balance of Triple M. gone?

Robert J. Mammola

The tyrant is keeping that from being shown by not making her appointed trustee follow federal rules. Remember, the reason for selling our home was there was not enough money to pay the City of Revere. How could that be if the co-owners' proceeds from Triple M. are in escrow by court order? By federal law, taxes, and liens are a priority. (They must be paid first.) Also, we can't forget the US trustee's motion. If an agreement is made with the Chapter 7 thief (trustee), he can't be paid until a plan has been approved. Well, I guess it's time to show the saboteurs just what they are. Simply put, in East Cambridge talk, they are lowlife thieves "So low, they stand tall talking under the belly of a snake.". My courage, conviction, resolve, and most important, my Christian faith are insurmountable. To all of those who enjoyed the pain and heartache they inflicted on my family, hold on; it's the Mammolas' turn at bat. I, Robert J. Mammola, on December 3, 2012, gave the (you're right) *tyrant* (judge,), her former partner the Chapter 7 trustee, his attorney, his law firm, the bank's attorney, and his law firm a Christmas present, which I filed in federal district court under the supreme law of the land (the Constitution of the United States of America). This lawsuit delineates and precisely lays out every law each of the defendants has violated, every article of the US Constitution, every amendment of the Constitution, and every federal law in the amount of $100,000,000. It is Robert J. Mammola, plaintiff, versus R. the tyrant (judge) and other defendants. Now each of the defendants has twenty-one days to respond, except the judge, who has sixty days to respond. I have referred to the judge as a tyrant through this chain of events for good reason. Honor was impossible in this courtroom. *Honor* is a title of respect and honesty, which breeds justice. You won't find justice in this judge's courtroom. Now with the lawsuit being filed, every injustice that has been allowed over the past three years in the judge's court is now public record. I know she believes she is above the law and has a lot of power in the Boston judicial system. I hope she and every one of the defendants haven't forgotten about the Supreme Court. Each defendant now has to answer each and every count as stated in the lawsuit. To a constitutional, honorable judge, under the pains and penalty of perjury, the first to answer was the attorney. In accordance with Federal Rule Civ. 7 and local rule 7.1, the judge moved to dismiss my complaint for failure to state a claim. This a joke, right? Or maybe he didn't read the suit. If so, he (the judge's attorney) couldn't really be from the Department of Justice. The attorney also stated that the suit was incorrectly served. That problem was solved when I presented the UPS tracking number. The attorney stated that the claims in my complaint against the judge consisted solely of acts that fell within the doctrine of absolute judicial immunity. He stated it had been held that "judges of courts of superior or general jurisdiction are not liable to civil action for their judicial acts, even when such acts are in excess of their jurisdiction, and are alleged to have been done maliciously or corruptly. (This is a lengthy law, but I'll take just the section that the Supreme Court intentionally put in to cover the law. He, the judge's attorney, must have missed this section. "Judges are protected by absolute judicial immunity for all acts performed in an official capacity where the act itself is not "expressly prohibited by existing law" (*expressly*, meaning "for a specific purpose"; *prohibited* by law, rule, or authority; and *existing*, meaning "in operation at the time"). By statute (law) of the US Constitution, the supreme law of the land, Article 1 (c1.8.18), in part, powers granted by the Constitution, Article iii (3.1.1.), in part, judges must demonstrate good behavior, Article vi (6.2), in part, judges will be bound by this supreme law, Amendment 1 (c1), in part, petition the government for a redress of grievances, and Amendment 14, in part "no state may take away any person's life, liberty, or property without proper operation of the law (or equal protection of the law). These are just a few of the violations to mention. But at the end of the book will be the full text of the US Constitution. Keep in mind at the trial by jury, we have every document that each one of these oath takers who swore to pursue justice filed in motion form (under the pains and penalty of perjury) in court. Think back to October 29, 2010, when the judge in open court said, just four days after having my Chapter 7 case moved to her court, "I won't make any gratuitous observations, but I've never thought Seta Mammola was anything but a straw for her husband" (factual evidence of judicial misconduct). Judicial action taken without any arguable legal basis and without giving notice and an opportunity to be heard to the party adversely affected is far worse than simple error or abuse of discretion; it's an abuse of judicial power that is "prejudicial to the effective and expeditious administration of the business of the courts." Section 455 of title 28 governs the disqualification of federal judges, including bankruptcy judges, from acting in particular case. Of relevance to this particular case are the requirements that a judge shall disqualify him- or herself in "any proceeding in which his impartiality might reasonably be questioned" or " where he has a personal bias or prejudice concerning a party" Title 28 USC § 455 455 (a) and (b) (1)). The judge appointed the Chapter 11 trustee (sua sponte). According to Title 11 USC § 1104the US trustee is required to consult with the parties in interest prior to the appointment. Very important are the qualifications, and if the appointed trustee is a disinterested person when a trustee is appointed, he or she must disclose any possible conflict of interest that could exist. Remember, Seta wanted to have a court hearing regarding the Chapter 7 trustee's claim I was a 50 percent owner. The Chapter 11 trustee said, "If you push that issue, the judge will convert Seta's Chapter 11 to a Chapter 7 case liquidation." The Chapter 11 trustee was in court on the same day she was appointed to Seta's Chapter 11 case on a different Chapter 7 case opposing the attorneys who made up our trust. I'm sure she did not that day, but a week after her appointment, my daughter Diane and I went over all the trust documents, checking accounts and tenants as to what each of the rents were. The plan was laid out at the 341 meeting with the US trustee. That week, the Chapter 11 trustee knew who the trust attorneys were. At that time, she had a fiduciary obligation to disclose those facts, but she did not. The judge appointed a Chapter 7 trustee to Seta's Chapter 11 case with zero experience and even fewer qualifications. This was no accident. The Chapter 7 trustee would not have been able to put his scheme or artifice in play with a honest and competent Chapter 11 trustee. Now do you get the picture who's running the courtroom? Think about the results in a sequence of events if an honest and competent Chapter 11 trustee was appointed—no fraudulent claim allowed from the Chapter 7 trustee of my case, no change in the plan laid out at the 341 meeting by the debtor, Triple M. would have sold as condos for a total of $4,650,000 and net profit of $2,500,000, the bankruptcy case would have been over in one year or less, no loss of 14 Yeamans Street Realty Trust or the three family condos, and no loss of 10 Yeamans Street Realty Trust with twenty-six apartments and five stores, and no loss of our family home of twenty-five years. My wife and I would be together—the whole family actually. That I can't get into. Back to the judge's attorney from the district attorney's department who represents you and me as US citizens. He stated both cases, Chapter 7 and Chapter 11, were proceeding under a (theory) that Seta and I were the owners of the trusts and was attempting to collaterally attack the judge's decisions through this suit, by alleging that the judge's actions have amounted to judicial misconduct. What happened to justice or fact-finding, making decisions based on factual documentation? The judge took an oath, "I take this obligation freely, without any mental reservation or purpose of evasion." *Evasion* is the act of evading something (in this case, the facts). The undeniable truth is if the documents were examined as to who the true owners were, the judge's former partner's fraudulent claim would have been exposed. The final point as to the judge's attorney, she makes reference to Local Rule 7.1, requiring counsel to confer. "As such, the rule is inapposite. Alternatively, because the plaintiff is pro se, the United States requests leave to file this motion without a conference." The assistant US attorney said this. Unless I'm wrong, the US Attorney operates as part of the government (c1.8, 18): "To make all laws which are necessary and proper for executing the powers listed above and all other powers granted by the Constitution to the government of the United States or to any department or officer of it." Article 6.2, says, in part, "Judges in every state will be bound by this supreme law, regardless of anything in any state law or state constitution. Amendment 1, in part, says, it is allowed for "people to petition the government for a redress of Grievances." Amendment 14 says, "No state may deny any person under its authority the equal protection of the laws.

Enough of the judge's attorney, after all, he is an assistant. Give him time. The US Constitution is a lot to learn.

The Chapter 7 trustee, the man with a plan, is a perfect example. When power corrupts, it tends to corrupt absolutely. The first time I met this trustee, I was impressed by how he studied the information I supplied, in particular the documents from the bank, being their minutes of a bank meeting regarding a specific loan approval. With this document in hand, he asked, "Where did you get this?"

I replied, "My attorney, through discovery in a lawsuit with the bank."

He replied, "Do you know how important this is?"

My reply was, "Yes, very much so."

The Chapter 7 trustee said, "We are going to continue this meeting at another time. I'll have a notice sent to you. That's it for today."

I went home and told my wife and daughters what had taken place, and I felt good about it. Now someone was going to see what a screwing we were getting from the bank. That, I truly believed, was where he was coming from, but the bank saw a chance to really fuck all over Bob Mammola, and they jumped on it. They told the Chapter 7 trustee I was a 50 percent owner of all the trust. That was the end of that trustee looking for justice. That thief saw all the money in equity in all the trusts. No way he wasn't getting his pound of flesh (money). The bank misled the Chapter 7 trustee just to cause me a barrel of trouble in my Chapter 7 bankruptcy case, and they did just that—a whole world of trouble, even to the point it backfired on the bank. The Chapter 7 trustee's former partner was the judge in my wife's Chapter 11 case. She had no problem openly assisting the Chapter 7 trustee in his scheme or artifice. My Chapter 7 case was in another honorable judge's court. When the bank filed a motion to foreclose on my two pieces of property—10 Milano Avenue in Revere, Massachusetts, and the Hamilton Property—the Chapter 7 trustee filed a motion to object but at the last minute. For some reason, he removed his objection. But surprise! The Chapter 7 trustees' attorney filed a notice of appearance in Seta's chapter 11 case, the same morning. The big question is why was this done on October 13, 2010? A week earlier, the judge, the Chapter 7 trustee's former partner, for no legal reason, spontaneously appointed a trustee in Seta's chapter 11 case (sua sponte)—a Chapter 7 trustee in a Chapter 11 case. The Constitution refers to this type of move as usurpation. Usurpation is taking a position of power by force or illegally (without just cause). This Chapter 7 trustee's was handling a Chapter 11 case of this magnitude without any experience or qualification; it's no wonder between the Chapter 7 trustee of my bankruptcy case and his scheme or artifice to sabotage, along with the appointed Chapter 7 trustee as a Chapter 11 trustee in the Seta's case, that her chapter 11 bankruptcy case to reorganize turned into Chapter 11 destruction. Then on October 29, 2010, the judge made her biased position very clear, as to how she had a predetermination regarding my Chapter 7 case. Remember the oath ("without any purpose of evasion," the action of evading something—the truthful facts). Now the attorney for the Chapter 7 trustee of my Chapter 7 case had a three-hour-plus deposition of me. Under oath, at that deposition, I supplied all factual documentation as to all the realty trust, including who the beneficiaries were in 1994 when the trust originated and still were at that date in September 2010. I also supplied documents with regards to 34 Mammola Way in Medford, Massachusetts, the realty trust that was formed in 1994. It clearly showed my wife and our daughter Michela as 50 percent beneficiaries (owners). A document that showed that I, as the property manager, had power of attorney, signed by the beneficiaries, gave me authority to make all pertinent business and daily decisions. The attorney for the Chapter 7 trustee actually believed his statements were absolutely privileged. One would think this attorney just fell out of the sky or he missed the class regarding rule 11 of the federal rules of civil procedure and similar state rules requiring that an attorney perform a due diligence investigation concerning the factual basis for any claim or defense. Jurisdictions differ on whether a claim or defense can be frivolous if the attorney acted in good faith. The Chapter 7 trustee's attorney, after a three-hour-plus deposition, filed a motion in total contradiction of the factual documents that I supplied and testified to under oath in the deposition. Here are just a few of his, as he put it, pieces of overwhelming proof.

He stated that I put 34 Mammola Way in a sham trust in March 1988. In my wife's and our daughter's names, I met my wife in September 1988. We were married in May 1989. Our daughter Michela was born on August 4, 1990. He claims I set up a trust in someone's name and in a baby's name two years before her birth, not knowing if I was going to be blessed with another child. Get this; he claims I knew two years in advance I was going to have another girl, three daughters. Tell me God doesn't have a sense of humor. The trustee's attorney claimed I had total disregard for the trust by-laws, that I simply did whatever I wanted with regard to the trust property. At the deposition, I gave him, along with the other documents, a copy of a durable power of attorney to me, signed by all the beneficiaries. That document made him a liar or just stupid. He stated that all the financial statements were certified (officially confirmed in a formal statement). The financial statements were all handwritten by me (not certified, as he states). This same attorney claims "alleged irregularities." Where I come from, they are out and out *lies*.

Another claim (not facts, just him running off with his mouth), was that I was using all the money from the trust for myself. The Chapter 11 trustee filed a motion in court (December 6, 2010), stating that the debtor Seta had been paying all bills to run the trust properly. She must have gotten a bite in her bum, not good for the Chapter 7 trustee. He was not supposed to be truthful; it was not good for his scheme or artifice. I'm certainly not pinning any medals on her. She simply screwed up. It certainly can't be both ways; the bills were being paid or I was taking all the money. Need I say any more? Remember, he was the Chapter 7 attorney. The Judge wasn't going to check her former partner's motions. And she didn't remember my motion for clarification and declaratory relief. This same attorney filed a motion of objection. He stated it was incoherent. I can believe that the truth will always bite his kind in the ass. (He couldn't tell the truth if it served the purpose.) The attorney for the Chapter 7 trustee also stated that the plaintiff had to state facts that "possess enough heft to show that he is entitled to relief" (by strict pleading requirements of rule 9, which simply put, states that any claim must be pled with particularity—specification of time, place, and content—so according to him, a motion filed in court must not conform, even though it is filed under the pains of the penalty of perjury. That little lawsuit I filed, it's got to suck, because all his peers, because of it being on public court record, know how deceitful, dishonest, and ruthless he really is. His type could care less. I'll bet the Boston bar of overseers won't be impressed when they receive it or see it on Boston and CNN. The Chapter 7 trustee was pulling all the strings from behind the scenes. Now it was just to completely break my family. Unlike his attorney, he could care less, who knows he's a sneak and a thief. All he wants is his pound of flesh. Some of the federal rules he has violated are criminal. When proven in a jury trial, he will face criminal charges and will pay for all the wrong he has caused; depending on the rule, it's five or twenty years in jail. I'm sure he is laughing about my lawsuit, simply because he is a big unfeeling piece of (?) and he believes with his former partner, the judge. (You thought I forgot about her, hah! Surprise, I'm in this for the long run, no matter where, who, how long, or what it takes to make all of them pay.) They have one big problem. I have never been taught how to quit, only to survive no matter what. That's an East Cambridge promise. The only thing we have and most important in our lives is our good name. That's the only thing we leave behind. I am seventy years old. I have worked hard to build a good, honest, and reliable Christian reputation over the past fifty-plus years. These saboteurs have another think coming if they think that I am just going to turn the other cheek. Never. The bank's attorney was crying I was attacking him and his law firm because they represent the bank. That's just the type of maneuver (carefully planned scheme) they have played through this whole entire scheme or artifice. I clearly filed my suit, based on the deception and the distortion of the facts each attorney from the same firm played through *motions* filed in superior court and bankruptcy court. Then when a citizen of the United States, under the protection of the supreme law of the land (the US Constitution), fights back, they lawyer up and cry. Any claims or statements they make are protected by absolute immunity and litigation privilege. I truly believe, at this point, after studying and acquiring some knowledge of the US Constitution (the supreme law of the land), none of the law-enforcement—excuse me, all of these defendants—have not read, do not remember, or simply do not care about what it stands for—that being freedom of life, liberty, and the pursuit of *happiness*. When studying the Constitution in its entirety, I learned the framers collectively hammered out each and every word, over and over again, until they covered and barred every chance to misinterpret the intent of the law. The framers of the Constitution, from all the federalist writings, settled on seven articles. Twelve years later (1787), they ratified the Constitution and added the twenty-seven amendments, the first ten of which are the Bill of Rights. The framers did this to form a more perfect union. I'm sorry; I'm getting to the point very soon. The First Amendment states the people have the right to petition the government to redress any grievances they have caused. The Fourteenth Amendment states that no state may make or enforce any law that diminishes the privileges or freedom of citizens of the United States. No state may take away any person's life, liberty, or property without the proper operation of law. Thanks to the framers, this BS about immunity litigation privilege, that is a state law. You just read the Constitution. It clearly tells them to stick it. Article 6.2 makes it very clear that judges in every state will be bound by this supreme law, regardless of anything in any state law or state constitution. So let's be clear; judges can't make any ruling contrary to the US Constitution. The judge's insolence is clearly displayed by her position and her action. Attorneys can't twist the laws to fit their needs. Sad to say, they have been more often than we want to believe. The Supreme Court has allowed attorneys to use what's called precedent as a substitute law or statute (an earlier legal case that's used as an example). Article 1.1.1 of the Constitution says, "All of the lawmaking powers granted by this agreement will be entrusted to a congress of the United States. Congress will consist of a Senate and a House of Representatives." Nothing in that article mentions that the Supreme Court can substitute or make any laws (such as precedents) that violate the Constitution. I had to lay these parts of the Constitution out at this time, for what is to follow from the bank's own attorney. He stated, "First circuit holds a pro-se litigant to a standard of pleading less stringent than that for lawyers. This cannot be taken to mean that pro-se complaints are held to no standard at all. Also pro se can't venture into the realm of the fantastic." The attorney continued, "[Under] Massachusetts law, an attorney's statements are absolutely privileged. Privileged does not mean they may disregard rule 11 as to due diligence as to the facts in a case." His client misled the Chapter 7 trustee, regarding me being a 50 percent owner of all the trusts. (Are we to believe lies are privileged?) The attorney stated Federal Rule civ. P.9 (b), which requires that such claims the "circumstances constituting fraud" be pled "with particularity" as to time, place, and content of an alleged false representation. (I guess a motion is not factual enough.) I don't know when the bank's attorney misled the Chapter 7 trustee behind closed doors. The bank's attorney, in a motion filed January 17, 2011, in court stated the court would have an abundance of caution as to the Chapter 7 trustee's assertion that I was a 50 percent owner of all the trusts. At this point, the bank's attorney violated Title 18 USC Subsection 1519 by changing the bank's position in bankruptcy court as to me not being the owner of record at the registry of deeds. Yet in superior court, the bank stated I was a 50 percent owner.

The federal law being violated here was judicial estoppel, when a litigant takes a position in one court on the same matter and then changes his or her position in another court. The bank's attorney continued the Chapter 7 trustee was making a "veil piercing" or "alter ego" claim so as to pierce the trust, but conveniently, the bank left only after the chapter 7 trustee was misled by the bank and their attorneys. The attorney went on to say the complaint failed to identify the specific statements that were claimed to have been false and fraudulent. Nor was there any claim of reliance by the plaintiff, which is an essential part of a prima facie case of fraud. The attorney's counselor must not have read, seen, or given any credence to the Chapter 7 motion filed on January 18, 2011, in response to the bank's motion of January 17, 2011. The chapter 7's motion makes it very clear that it was the bank's attorney who mislead the chapter 7 trustee regarding my 50 percent ownership in all the trusts. (Remember that trick behind closed doors that backfired on the bank?) All of the motions filed clearly state a time, a place, and content. Did the bank's attorney's counselor miss those facts with regard to rule 9's requirement of specification of the time, place, and content? The counselor summed up his motion to dismiss by stating my claim was only against his clients in count 4. That's BS. In count 4, his clients were barred by the absolute litigation privilege. I don't want to be redundant, but out-and-out lies are not covered by absolute litigation privilege. It's plain to see it didn't take long for his clients to throw all the other defendants under the bus. Just imagine what will take place in a jury trial. Enough of the fourth attorney's BS. This attorney is from the same law firm that represents both Boston banks. He has continued to file in motion form (now in federal district court) the same scheme or artifice of deception, which this gem of a counselor calls "alleged irregularities." All these attorneys have done all of this, as he states with the client's authority and in good faith as to its grounds. Get this—as officers of the court in the pursuit of justice under oath. My suit has been filed. The defendants all have filed a motion to dismiss. I have filed a motion in opposition to their motion to dismiss. Now we wait for the federal honorable judge to set a court date for a jury trial (a jury trial by right, as per the intent of the framers of the US Constitution, in Article 1.8.4) to establish standard rules for becoming a naturalized citizen and establish standard laws about bankruptcy throughout the United States. Article 1.8.18, in part, makes all laws that are necessary and proper for executing the powers listed: Article 1.10. 1 (d) says no state may pass any law that interferes with private contracts; Article 3. 1 says the judges, both of the Supreme and inferior courts, shall hold their office during good behavior. Article 5. 1 (a) says the Congress, whenever two-thirds of both houses shall deem it necessary, shall propose amendments to the Constitution. Article 6. 2 states that the Constitution shall be the supreme law of the land and the judges in every state shall be bound by anything in the Constitution, laws of any state contrary notwithstanding.

Amendment 1 says, "Congress shall make no laws prohibiting the people the right to peaceably assemble and to petition the government for a redress of grievances." Amendment 7 states, "In suits at common law, where the Value in controversy shall exceed twenty dollars, the right of trial by jury shall be preserved." Amendment 14 states, "All persons born or naturalized in the United States, and subject to the jurisdiction thereof, are citizens of the United States and of the state wherein they reside. No state shall make or enforce any law which shall abridge the privileges or Immunities of citizens of the United States; nor shall any state deprive any person of Life, Liberty, or Property, without Due Process of the Law; nor deny to any person within its jurisdiction the equal protection of the laws." (Big Bob's and Michela's, May 4, 2014!) These are the precise articles and amendments of the US Constitution that the saboteurs blatantly and purposely violated by abuse of power for greed of money without any regard as to the devastation it caused a very close, happy, and successful family. James Madison said, "Power tends to corrupt, and absolute power corrupts absolutely."

Recently, my daughters have filed in federal district court a suit against the two Boston banks for unfair and deceptive business practices and violation of banking regulation per the FDIC cease and desist order of July 14, 2009 and a suit against the Chapter 11 trustee for breach of contract and the following violations of her fiduciary obligations: 1) Federal Rule regarding, subsection 322, the trustee assumes control over the assets and business operations of the debtor (only assets of the debtor; the trustee is an independent third party who "steps into the shoes of the debtor's management and becomes a fiduciary with an obligation of fairness to all parties in the case) to safeguard the assets of the debtor. 2) Subsection 321(a), the trustee must be competent to perform the statutory duties set out in subsection 1106. 3) Rule Subsection 324(a) mandates removal of a trustee to the extent that the trustee is not complying with fiduciary obligations. 4) Subsection 1106 (5) says if a purpose would be served, one must examine proof of claims and object to the allowance of any claim that is improper. 5) The Chapter 11 debtor in possession (DIP) is authorized to borrow funds and a super priority lien may be obtained ($2,300,0000, the trustee refused). 6) Title 18 U.S.C. Subsection 1519 says, "Whoever knowingly alters, destroy, mutilates, conceals, covers up, falsifies, or makes a false entry in any record, document, or tangible object with the intent to impede, obstruct, or influence the investigation or proper administration of any matter within the jurisdiction of any department or agency of the United States or any case filed under title 11 or in relation to or contemplated of any such matter or case, shall be fined under this title, imprisoned not more than twenty years, or both. 7) The Chapter #11 trustee refused to address my question as to my spousal rights to my wife's share of the sale of our home. Federal Rule 363 (j) says thus the costs of the sale are prorated among the co-owner or spouse and the estate, next in order to distribute the sale proceeds "according to the interest of such spouse or co-owner and of the estate"; as required by Section 363 (j), the trustee or court must look to applicable nonbankruptcy law (generally state law) or contracts to determine the interests of the debtor and nondebtors relative to each other It should be replaced with: 1-2 Collier Family Law and the Bankruptcy Code P 2.06

The judge appointed the Chapter 11 trustee. Once she accepted the appointment, she became a fiduciary. The court forced the debtor into placing her utmost trust and confidence to manage and protect property or money in her. In this relationship, one person has an obligation to act for another's benefit. Under this scheme of artifice, the trustee's obligation was to the Chapter 7 trustee. A fiduciary obligation never existed between the debtor (Seta) and her court-appointed Chapter 11 trustee. Had the Chapter 11 trustee been appointed according to the Reform Act of 1978, as is required by Federal Rule, she would have been honest and competent to handle a Chapter 11 case. The Chapter 11 trustee would have answered only to the US trustee. The trustee would have been trustworthy and, most important, would have followed the debtor's plan as laid out at the 341 meeting with the US trustee. The debtor's plan to sell Triple M. as condos as a business plan would have worked out perfectly. The Chapter 7 trustee would have never been allowed to make his fraudulent claim without factual evidence. The existing tenants who put down deposits to buy their existing rental units still have not been paid (a total of $23,000). My family would have realized a profit in excess of $2,500,000. We would not have had to sell our home under the pretense they would get to keep 10 Yeamans Street, a thirty-one rental property in Revere, Massachusetts. The trustee would not be illegally taking my spousal share of the debtor's proceeds. In Massachusetts, a married couple own 50 percent of all tangible property. Our daughter would not have had to twice skip a semester at Suffolk University. With all the heartache, turmoil, and stress, she still maintained a dean's list status.

The trustee would not have held hostage $150,000 of our daughter's proceeds from the sale of our home for over fourteen months, which would have eliminated the interruption of her education. She would not have lost two pieces of income property in an extremely profitable real estate market for buyers. It's been over a year and a half, and the trustee is still holding over $40,000 through her own scheme to build an illegal bill against those funds, with the judge's blessing to do so (Ricky's bill was eliminated) with total disregard as to bankruptcy and federal rules as to co-owners' specific rights and duties and the obligation of a Chapter 11 Trustee. The $80,000 in credit cards that was to be paid by the Triple M. sale, the Chapter 11 trustee has no intentions of paying, totally ignoring the US trustee's motion as to what the trustee intends to pay the credit cards and what the trustee's intentions are as to the other issues. As I stated, the lawsuits all have been filed in federal district court. The regional criminal coordinator for the criminal enforcement unit has been notified as to all the criminal violations. The Federal Bureau of Investigation has been notified. The Boston bar of overseers has been notified. The *Boston Globe* is very interested as to the scheme of conspiracy.

My family now has (unlike in the judge's court) a voice—the Constitution of the United States of America, (the supreme law of the land). The federal district court's honorable judges have no time for any bias. Their (thank God Almighty) only concern is justice, as to the intent of the framers of the Constitution of the United States. (God bless America.)

Robert J. Mammola

The following are questions for a bankruptcy consultant: Is the trustee required to follow what's laid out at the 341 meeting? Did the existing tenants' deposits to buy as condos preempt the trustee's change of the plan laid out at the 341 meeting? If the trustee sells the debtor's property for less than fair market value, is she responsible? Does the trustee legally have control of co-owners' shares of the funds? Did the trustee have a legal obligation to examine the Chapter 7 claim, rule S.S. 1106 (a) 4 (a) required to file for an investigation, for facts as to fraud, dishonesty, or a cause of action available to the estate? 11 USC § 1106 (a) 28 USC § 95911 u. S. C. S. S. 1106(a). Finally, 28 U.S.C. Subsection 959 says the trustee may be sued without leave of the court of appointment (shall not deprive a litigant of his or her right to a trial by jury). U.S.C. Subsection 345 says the trustee must protect and preserve estate assets and any criminal actions must be reported to the assistant US trustee or the criminal coordinator of the criminal enforcement unit, the US attorney, and the FBI. U.S.C. Subsection 152 (2) makes a false oath (in a motion) (4) makes a false proof of claim (6) to obtain money (10) 18 Subsection 155 knowingly and fraudulently enter into an agreement with another party in interest or its attorney (11) 18 U.S.C. added 18 U.S.C. Subsection 1519 (3) makes a false or Fraudulent claim (before or after filing) (12). Does the trustee have a claim to the entire proceeds of the married debtor's sale of property (the family's home)? See *In re Coombs*, and *In re Persky* the Court and Supreme Court opinions (July 6, 2014). For the home in question, the debtor owned 50 percent, being married. Does not 50 percent of the debtor's share belong to her spouse? The trustee didn't abide by the US trustee's objection (May 5, 2011), paying the Chapter 7 trustee if an agreement was reached.

The credit card payments were laid out at the 341 meeting. 14) (11 U. S. C. S.S. 1104 appointment of a trustee.) The appointment of a Chapter 11 trustee is generally considered an extraordinary remedy. Thus, although the provision is mandatory, a finding of sufficient cause for the appointment of a trustee is within the discretion of the bankruptcy judge. While the US Code grants the court authority to approve the US trustee's appointment of a Chapter 11 trustee, the court may not usurp the appointment process or otherwise seek to supplant the judgment exercised by the US Trustee during the process (compromises and settlements, bankruptcy rule 9019). To obtain this approval, the trustee must show that the settlement is in the best interest of the estate and that notice of the compromise has been served upon creditors so they have an opportunity to review the proposed settlement and object. Generally, courts give substantial deference to the trustee's business judgment in such matters. This trustee has absolutely zero business sense. She had no idea as to how to handle the closing of the sale of Triple M. Proof is in the HUD sheet. The property was to be sold as is. The trustee gave the buyers over $20,000 in gifts. Neither have the credit card creditors been properly notified or notified at all. According to U.S.C. Section 363 (use, sale, or lease of property), sales, large and small, are ever present in bankruptcy practice, so a rudimentary understanding of section 363 (j) and its related provisions couldn't hurt. What's more, these provisions underscore the burdens attendant to certain forms of co-ownership of property and, accordingly, why estate-planning and other professionals have gravitated toward trusts in lieu of common-law estates.

In a sale to which 11 USC § 363 (g) (h)363 (g) or (h) of this section applies, the trustee shall distribute to the debtor's spouse or the co-owner of such property, as the case may be, and to the estate. The proceeds of such a sale, less the costs and expenses, do not include any compensation of the trustee of such sale, according to the interests of such spouse or co-owners. The effect of a 363 (h) sale would be to deprive the non-debtor spouse of two interests—possessory and the survivorship rights.

THIS QUOTE OF JUDGE YOUNG IS TAKEN FROM A TOTALLY DIFFERENT
BANKRUPTCY CASE. BUT IN MY OPIION ITS PRECISELY WHAT I HAVE WITNESSED IN BOTH MY [RJM] CHAPTER 7 CASE AND MY WIFE [SRM]

CHAPTER 11 CASE.

JUDGE YOUNG'S harshest criticisms were for the LAWYER involved;

> "After 43 years at the bar, the saddest thing about this case is the conduct of the LAWYERS all the LAWYERS. A careful reading of the briefs in this case reveals only a singly recognition that counsel did anything amiss in their misrepresentations to the bankruptcy court. There's blame aplenty, of course. each one blaming everyone else--- including the hapless bankrupt homeowner... How is it that our profession, the legal profession, which could have and should have strongly counseled against the self-interested excesses that set up the collapse-- instead has eagerly aided and abetted those very excesses? How could WE [all of us who profess to be lawyers] have fallen so low.

I told you how fortunate Paul and I were with the move our dedicated parents made to make it possible for us to finish our high school education at Lexington High. I, Robert J. Mammola, will leave you saboteurs with this thought, taught to me and my brother Paul by those brilliant teachers at Lexington High School in Lexington, Massachusetts. Funny the shot heard around the world was fired in Lexington and Concord, Massachusetts, in the year 1776 by the minuteman, who just happened to be the people who started the revolution to overthrow the existing government and had a great deal to do with the framing of the supreme law of the land, that being the Constitution of the United States of America, which all you saboteurs blatantly violated. The conservative movement has sought to alter the basic precepts of constitutional law. You must first enable the government to control the governed. In the next place, oblige it to control itself. (This is worth repeating.)

I leave you with this, which was taught to me by my English teacher at Lexington high school in my senior year (1963.) It has served me very well throughout my adult life. These pearls of wisdom are by William Shakespeare.

Soliloquy
"To Be or Not to Be"
From *Hamlet* Act 3, Scene 1

To be or not to be, that is the question, whether tis nobler in the Mind to suffer the slings and arrows of outrageous fortune, or to take arms against a sea of troubles, and by opposing end them; To die, to sleep no more; and by a sleep to say we end the heartache, and the thousand natural shocks that flesh is heir to. 'Tis a Consummation devoutly to be wished. To die to sleep, to sleep, Perchance to dream; ay, there's the rub, for in that sleep of Death, what dreams may come, must give us pause, there's the Respect that makes calamity of so long life; for who would bear the whips and scorns the oppressor's wrong, the proud man's Contumely, the pangs of despised love, the law's delay, the Insolence of office, that patient merit of the unworthy takes when he himself might his quiet us make with a bare bodkin? Who would these fardels bear, to grunt and sweat under a weary life, but that the dread of something after death, the undiscovered country from whose bourn no traveler returns, puzzles the will and makes us rather bear those ills we have, than fly to others that we know not of? Thus conscience does make cowards of us all, and thus the native hue of resolution is sicklied o'er with the pale cast of thought, and enterprises of great pitch and movement. With this regard their currents turn away, and lose the name of action.

The fight for Due Process Continues.

THIS IS THE LATEST MOTION FILED
SEPTEMBER 20.2016. THAT WILL BE HEARD ON DECEMBER 1, 2016

UNITED STATES BANKRUPTCY COURT
DISTRICT OF MASSACHUSETTS
EASTERN DIVISION

In re:	)	Chapter 7
	)	
SETA R. MAMMOLA	)	Case No. 10-15148
	)	
DEBTOR	)	
	)	
	)	
ROBERT J. MAMMOLA	)	
V.	)	
Kathleen Dwyer et al.	)	
	)	

ROBERT J. MAMMOLA'S RESPONSE TO NOTICE OF
TRUSTEE'S FINAL
REPORT AND APPLICATIONS FOR COMPENSATION [N F R]

This document is to represent Robert J Mammola's formal response to the Trustee's final Report and Applications for Compensation (N.F.R)

This motion is twofold; first request is that Judge Feeney Recuse herself due to the fact that she could potentially hold a conflict of interest. It would be difficult to accept the idea she would not be acting impartially given her personal relationship with her friend and former partner Harold Murphy. Factual evidence to this claim is listed below. It became evidence of Judge Feeney's bias opinion from the time she moved RJM's Chapter (7) case to her courtroom on 10/25/2010. It is made remarkably clear on 10/29/2010 just four days later when she states verbatim in open court, "I won't make any gratuitous observations, but I've never thought Seta Rose Mammola was anything but a [straw] for her husband.

The [straw man tactic] is essentially to take some small part of an arguer's position, and then treat it as if that represented his larger position, even though it is not really representative of that larger position;
Second request is for the Removal of Kathleen P. Dwyer and to request the court to appoint a special investigative Trustee to reconcile all funds received and paid out from the day she was appointed Trustee by this Court over SRM's Chapter (11) case to the present date. This was a financially strong Chapter (11) case with approximately $12,000,000 in holdings, $3,450,000 in mortgages and back taxes of $250,000 which accrued due to renovations and the transition process of Malden and Revere Properties into Condominiums. The Debtor in possession (SRM) on 9/27/2010 secured $2,300,000 through the court appointed accountant that charged $6,000 for securing these funds only a week before the court appointed Kathleen Dwyer as trustee Sua Sponte; There was no hearing, or just cause as Federal Law requires.

JUDGE FEENEY'S, INJUSTICE ACTIONS AND LACK OF JUST ACTIONS.

Judge Feeney denied Robert J. Mammola his Constitutional rights, The right to know one's accuser and the evidence against one; the right to confront and cross-examine that person; the right to have decision based solely upon a record generated in open proceedings; as well as the right to present argument and evidence on one's own behalf.]

Having Robert J. Mammola's Chapter 7 Case moved to her court, October 25,
2010 That move made R.J.M. an interested party in the S.R.M. Chapter 11 Case. This move Insured her former partner Harold Murphy's successes in his scheme of artifice, Plan to knowingly violate Fed. R.S.S. 1519 by making his fraudulent claim R.J.M. Is a fifty percent owner of all three trusts.

Judge Feeney's Bias statement, on October 29, 2010.

> *"I won't make any gratuitous observations, but I've never thought Seta Rose Mammola was anything but a straw for her husband."*

The Deception of facts in regards to Triple M. RT. In Malden Ma.,10 & 14 Yeamans Street Realty Trust in Revere Ma. IN regards to the conflicting motions of ownership of the Trusts that is clearly stated by this Courts former partner Harold Murphy and East Boston Savings Bank's Attorney J. Liston. Which this Court took no action to resolve the true ownership of the three Trusts. This Court just kept delaying the hearing of true ownership till the presiding Judge's former partner Harold Murphy and Kathleen Dwyer the trustee in S.R.M. Chapter 11 case were able to force the non- debtors into a forced stipulation agreement to pay Harold Murphy off, which would allow the sale of Triple M. to go through] Judge Feeney allowed her former partner Harold Murphy to break procedure by not filing a proof of claim in the S.R.M. Chapter 11 Case.

October 13, 2010 Doc No.115 Attorney Lizotte's Notice of Appearance in SRM's Case.

December 6, 2010 Doc No. 134 PRIVATE SALE TRIPLE M. REALTY TRUST, MALDEN, MA., S.R.M. Chapter 11 Case as part of the Private Sale of Triple M. Realty Trust in Malden Ma.

The Agreement that the Non Debtors would leave their share of the Malden property $400,000 to fun the S.R.M. Chapter 11 plan which would pay Revere property Ten and Fourteen Yeamans St. taxes and liens. This Agreement, Contract, was signed by the Non--Debtors and Trustee Dwyer.
"COURTS HAVE FOUND THAT A CONTRACT MUST BE READ IN SUCH A WAY THAT NO PART OF THE AGREEMENT IS LEFT MEANINGLESS." See Starr v. Fordham, 420 Mass.

178, 190 [1995]; " In other words, contracts must be construed to give "reasonable effect". To I each provision obtained therein."

December 22, 2010 Doc No. 148 (Murphy) Objection by Chapter 7 Trustee of Robert Mammola to Motion for Relief from the Automatic Stay with Respect to 10 and 14 Yeamans Street, Revere, MA filed by Interested Party Harold B. Murphy Tr. Re: <u>128</u>
<u>December 22, 2010 Doc 149 (Murphy) OBJECTION BY CHAPTER 7 TRUSTEE OF ROBERT MAMMOLA TO CHAPTER 11 TRUSTEE'S MOTION FOR ORDER AUTHORIZING PRIVATE SALE OF PROPERTY re: Doc. 134.</u>

<u>Doc. 149 Pa. #1. MURPHY. States pending a determination of the respective ownership rights, [Yet that hearing did not take place.]</u>

> P. 2. In each case, R. Mammola ostensibly utilized his Wife, S. Mammola, as trustee and his three holders as beneficiaries.
>
> ALL THREE TRUSTS WERE IRREVOCABLE TRUSTE RECORDED IN
> THE REGISTRY OF DEEDS
>
> THE TRUSTEE WAS PROHIBITED FROM TAKING ANY MATERIAL ACTION WITH RESPECT TO THE
>
> TRUST PROPERTY WITHOUT THE WRITTEN DIRECTION OF THE BENEFICIARIES. IN PRACTICE, HOWEVER, THE PROVISIONS OF THE TRUSTS WERE ROUTINELY DISREGARDED. R. MAMMOLA TRATED THE PROPERTIES AS HIS OWN.
>
>> R.J.Mammola was not a trustee.
>> The beneficiaries gave R.J.Mammola written power of attorney.
>> THE INCORRECT TRUSTEE CERTIFICATES THAT WERE MISTAKENLY SIGNED BY SETA R. MAMMOLA AND ROBERT J. MAMMOLA WERE MADE UP BY THE BANK'S ATTORNEY. FORTUNATELY, ATTORNEY WILLIAM'S COT THE MISTAKE HE MADE AND RECORED THE RIGHT TRUSTEE CERTIFICATES AT THE REGISTRY OF DEEDS.
>
> [pa.] #3. Murphy states on or about December 6, 2010 Trustee Dwyer filed the sale Motion Doc.134. In addition December 22, 2010 Doc. 151 The Motion to sell Triple M. RT. K. Dwyer states, Net proceeds from the sale will total approximately. $400,000. [the taxes and liens for

Malden and Revere properties total were $250,000 at that time, which by agreement[CONTRACT] with the co-owners Non debtors and Trustee Dwyer were to be paid at the closing, the default would have been removed and the Chapter 11 would have ended.[Murphy's fraudulent claim stopped that by having his friend and former partner the presiding Judge put the $400,000 in Escrow until a hearing of factual ownership was held. [THAT HEARING NEVER TOOK PLACE.]

P.4 R. Mammola built the residence on or about 1985. On or about May 13, 1988, R. Mammola transferred the Residence to the 34 Mammola Way Realty Trust. Upon information and belief, S.Mammola and Michela Mammola are the alleged beneficiaries of the trust.

[ROBERT J. MAMMOLA and SETA R. STEPAINIAN MET IN SEPTEMBER 1988, MARRIED IN MAY 22, 1989. OUR DAUGHTER MICHELA R. MAMMOLA WAS BORN IN AUGUST 4, 1990.]

Murphy states at all times relevant thereto, R. Mammola utilized the trust

properties accounts to pay his personal expenses. [WHAT FACTS DOES MURPHY BASE THIS FRAUDULENT STATEMENT ON.]

[pa.] #5&6. Murphy states R.Mammola executed and delivered to Mt.Washington a Certified Personal Financial Statement.

[THE FINANCIAL STATEMENTS WERE HAND WRITTEN IN

THE. V.P.s Office at MT. Washington Bank by Robert J. Mammola.]

P.#7 Murphy states R. Mammola represented on numerous occasions his substantial ownership interest in the trust properties. [THE LAST PAGE

OF THE HAND WRITTEN FINANCIAL STATEMENT LIST EACH TRUST AND THE LEGAL OWNERS OF EACH TRUST.]

P. #8 Murphy states the overwhelming evidence supports a finding that the trust are a Sham and R. Mammola maintains an equitable interest of at least fifty percent [50%] in the trust properties. Murphy states that net proceeds be held by Trustee Dwyer pending a determination of ownership interest in such proceeds; and. [d] granting to the Trustee such other and further relief as the Court deems just and proper in the circumstances.

[HAD JUDGE FEENEY EXAMINED THE FACTUAL DOCUMENTS

SUPPLIED TO MURPHY BY ROBERT J. MAMMOLA AT HIS

DEPOSITIONS, THIS MOTION OF LIES AND DECEPTION WOULD

HAVE BEEN EXPOSED AS A SCHEME OF ARTIFICE.]

Judge Feeney denied, RJM'S MOTION OF DECLARATORY CLARIFICATION

Id. at 1760-61 (2009) (citations omitted). *"The Court then observed that, in determining whether the movant has met its burden, the "legal principles have been distilled into consideration of four factors":*

> *"(1) whether the stay applicant has made a strong showing that he is likely to succeed on the merits; (2) whether the applicant will be irreparably injured absent a stay; (3) whether issuance of the stay will substantially injure the other parties interested in the proceeding; and (4) where the public interest lies."* Id. at 1761 (citing Hilton v. Braunskill, 481 U.S. 770, 776 (1987)). See also

Philidor v. U. S. Att'y Gen., 384 Fed. Appx. 876, 878 (11th Cir. 2010).3 Of these four factors, the first two "are the most critical." Nken, 129 S. Ct. at 1761. Indeed, in his concurring opinion in Nken (joined in by Justice Scalia), Justice Kennedy stressed that both factors must be satisfied, Judge Feeney gave East Boston Savings Bank relief of stay on 14 Yeamans, taxes owed $14,750 with $400,000 of non-debtors funds in escrow until ownership rights hearing. [Which never took place.]
December 22, 2010 Doc No 151 (Dwyer) RESPONSE OF CHAPTER 11 TRUSTEE TO

MOTION OF EAST BOSTON SAVINGS BANK FOR RELIEF FROM STAY WITH RESPECT TO 10 AND 14 YEAMANS

STREET, REVERE, MA. K. Dwyer, States the Debtor did everything right from May through December 2010.

12] Judge Feeney BEING THE PRIMARY ADMINISTRATOR OF THE BANKRUPTCY
RULES never question K. Dwyer's filing of Court Doc. #42 on January 21, 2011 in R.J.M.
Chapter 7 case.
Spinner V. Nutt, 417 MASS [Beneficiary must show the parties entered into contract directly and primarily for Beneficiaries' Benefit.]. see Doc. #134 filed. 12--6--2010.

Judge Feeney, having two motions on her bench, Doc. #134 on December 6, 2010 in . S.R.M. Chapter 11 Case and Doc. #42 on January 21, 2011 in R.J.M. Chapter 7. Which totally contradict each other, [DID NOTHING in the pursuit of JUSTICE]

Judge Feeney stated the aggregate current value of all the properties is approximately. . $5,795,000.00 with a total mortgage count for $3,534,947.10. [This inaccurate value was provided by East Boston Savings Bank [EBSB]. In Doc.
#151 12/22/2010 filed by Chapter 11 Trustee Kathleen Dwyer clearly states, the appraiser is . is using the wrong figures]
[The Chapter 11 Trustee is marketing the 14 Yeamans Street properties in conjunction with the marketing of the 10 Yeamans Street property.]
[Total contrary to the Non -Debtors signed agreement [CONTRACT] in regards to their Non Bankruptcy funds of $400,000. see Doc. 134 & 151]
[IN ADDITION DOC. 151 PAGE #4 K. DWYER STATES MOREOVER, THE MALDEN. MUNICIPAL. LIENS AND CHARGES WILL BE PAID FROM THE SALE OF THE

PROPERTY WHICH IS SCHEDULED FOR JANUARY 31, 2011. THE NAMED BENEFICIARIES HAVE ASSENTED TO THE USE OF THE SURPLUS MALDEN PROCEEDS FOR PAYMENT OF REVERE MUNICIPAL LIENS AND CHARGES.]

[. K. DWYER NEVER TOOK THAT $400,000 IN ESCROW AND PAID OFF THE TOTAL REVERE TAXES AND LIENS AS THE CONTRACT REQUIRED.]

Judge Feeney refused to hear RJM motion filed January 19, 2011 along with three Affidavits from the Debtor and Co-Owners. [Denied to hear them, and denied RJM his CONSTITUTION Right to know one's accuser and the evidence against one; the right to confront and cross-examine that person; the right to have decision based solely upon a record generated in open proceedings; as well as the right to present argument and evidence on one's own behalf.]
Judge Feeney.   violated ARTICLE. VI.2 of the UNITED STATES CONSTITUTION,

> [in--part] states that Judges in every State Shall be bound thereby, any Thing in the Constitution or Laws of any State to the Contrary notwithstanding.

Judge Feeney states in her motion to dismiss RJM should not criticizing K. Dwyer for doing her job, IS STEALING $400,000 from MALDEN, $268,000 from MAMMOLA WAY and the EXCESS MONTHLY CASH FLOW from the RENTS EACH MONTH DOING HER JOB.

Judge Feeney, In her order to dismiss on April 9, 2015 page #33 [. *"The court concludes that Robert Mammola simply does not understand the consequence attendant to his personal bankruptcy and the failed Chapter 11 reorganization of his spouse, Seta Rose Mammola."*]. In answering that statement Robert J. Mammola will lay out the documented reasons for those result. But first I, MUST POINT out RJM would not have been forced into defending himself against Murphy's FRAUDULENT CRIMINAL CLAIM had this court followed Collier Family Law management of Co-Property. [When the property is a commercial or rental real property this may be relatively simple to arrange, with the trustee sharing income from the property.] The Co-Owners would have had money from their share of the rents to hire an attorney that would have stopped the injustice and improper appointment of Kathleen Dwyer. H.Murphy would have had to file a proof of claim. Section 541 [a][1] The Senate Amendment provided that Property of the Estate; does not include amounts held by the Debtor as a Trustee etc.

Had Judge Feeney. honored her oath, impart [I take this obligation freely, without any mental reservation [to have conflicted feelings.]or purpose of evasion;][Evade definition, to escape from by trickery or cleverness:] [a] through [m] that follows would not have transpired. a] Clearly not for Justice, RJM #7 case was moved to your court. b] The Bias statement you made on October 25,2010 made that very clear. c] Bankruptcy Rule calls for a hearing to show cause for appointing a Trustee. d] K. Dwyer was the most inept and certainly not qualified for a chapter 11 case.
The Conflict of Interest, which was discarded with Murphy and Dwyer on concurrent cases at the same time. f] Murphy never filed a proof of claim

This Court denied RJM motion filed 1/19/2011 Doc.149 and three affidavits.
Attorney Liston filed 1/ 17/2011 a motion for this court to have "an abundance of caution in regards To Murphy's fraudulent claim RJM WAS A 50% owner of all three trusts."

Murphy filed a motion on 1/ 18/ 2011 stating it was East Boston Savings Bank Attorney that told him RJM was a 50% owner of all three trust.

This Court order a hearing regarding the ownership rights of the three trust, Which never took place, just postponement after postponement etc.

This Court gave East Boston Savings Bank relief of stay on 14 Yeamans St. Taxes owed $14,750. [$400,000 of non-debtor's funs in escrow due to Murphy's Fraudulent claim that RJM owned 50% of all three trust.

With an unbiased Judge, a hearing as to who the true owners of all three trust would have eliminated all the costly motions and court time, and ended Murphy's Fraudulent Claim. m] This Court stated, The Forced Stipulation Agreement was good for both Bankruptcy cases, The "Stipulation" agreement negotiated to expedite the   "PRIVATE SALE" of Malden between the Debtor, the beneficiaries and Murphy was filed on April 11, 2011. (see In Re to Seta Rose Mammola) Doc No 228 and

Doc No. 229 "JOINT MOTION TO APPROVE" ...

The Court of Appeals has described the test to be used by Bankruptcy Courts called upon to approve or reject proposed compromises and settlements as follows: The bankruptcy judge has the authority to approve a compromise of a claim pursuant to Bankruptcy Rule 9019(a). The ultimate issue on appeal is whether the bankruptcy court abused its discretion when it approved the compromise, which is a process requiring the bankruptcy court to "assess and balance the value of the claim that is being compromised against the value to the estate of the acceptance of the compromise proposal." In re GHR Cos., 50 B.R. 925, 931 (Bankr. D. Mass. 1985) (quoting In re Boston & Providence R.R., 673 F.2d. 11, 12 (1st Cir. 1982)). The specific factors which a bankruptcy court considers when making this determination include: (i) the probability of success in the litigation being compromised; (ii) the difficulties, if any, to be encountered in the matter of collection; (iii) the complexity of the litigation involved, and the expense, inconvenience and delay attending it; and (iv) the paramount interest of the creditors and a proper deference to their reasonable views in the premise. In re Anolik, 107 B.R. 427, 429 (D. Mass. 1989). Jeffrey v. Desmond, 70 F.3d 183, 185 (1st Cir. 1995). The proposed settlement between the Trustees fairly balances "the value of the claims being compromised against the value to the estates of the acceptance of the compromise" THE SUPREME COURT HAD SAID,

" AN ACT OR PRACTICE IS DECEPTIVE IF IT POSSESSES A TENDENCY TO DECEIVE. "

April 5, 2011 Doc No. 226; "LIMITED OBJECTION OF THE UNITED STATES TRUSTEE TO JOINT DISCLOSURE" ... "Fails to provide adequate information regarding the proposed plan of reorganization"

Judge Feeney refuses to rule on the co-owner's motion to show where all funds have been paid out as Federal Rules require.
K. DWYER Violated FED. R. s.s.541re: no fees to the trustee from residential sale.
Dwyer took $268,000 from the sale of 34 Mammola.. Violating MAS. LAWS, FED. R. s.s. 522 in addition. Murphy took $25,000.

Section 363 [i] provides:

> After a sale of property to which subsection [g] or [h] of this section applies, the trustee shall distribute to the Debtor's Spouse or co-owners of such property, as the case may be, and to the Estate, the proceeds of such sale, less the cost and expenses, [not including any compensation of the trustee, of such sale, according to the interest of such spouse or co-owners, and the estate.] How an application of CPLR s.s. 5240 affects a s.s. 363 [h] sale [i]n view of state law [construing CPLR s.s. 5240 and the case in. Kathleen Dwyer also made Robert J. Mammola an interested party in his wife's Chapter 11 case.

By not objecting to Trustee Murphy of R.J.M.s Chapter 7 case. when he makes a fraudulent claim that R.J.M. was a 50% owner of all three trusts. Trustee Dwyer Violated her Fiduciary Duty FED. R. s.s. 345 to Protect the Assets of the Estate. By not invoking FED. R. 11 U.S.C. s.s. 704 [5] proof of claim. Harold Murphy never filed a proof of claim in the S.R.M. Chapter 11 Case.

K. Dwyer also in a motion [DOC.305 filed 6-13-2011] stated she would pay the Massachusetts Department of Revenue $26,000. What she paid was $4,400 and told R.J.M. if he did not take care of the total amount Judge Feeney would convert the Chapter 11 case to a Chapter 7. I made an agreement with the MDOR for them to take out $ 100 per month from my $805 social security monthly payment. I have paid a total of $5,400 to date. Dwyer stated in Court on 12--16--2014 she was holding $148,000. Now Dwyer wants to pay the MDOR $ 4,096.

Trustee Dwyer Violating s.s. 322 fairness to all parties [By the mishandling of the sale of Malden and the sale of our family home, there is no question that these funds are not property of the Estate which must be immediately return to the Non-Debtors]. [Section 541 [a][1] The Senate Amendment provided that Property of the Estate; does not include amounts held by the Debtor as a Trustee etc.]

JUDGE FEENEY'S Court order approving the sale of Malden was, property to be sold " AS IS " Dwyer gave the buyers an additional $19,000 off the Court order.

The Court order approving the sale of 34 Mammola Way was " AS IS & WHERE IS " Dwyer gave the buyers an additional $15,000 off the Court Order.

From Malden sale Dwyer put $400,000 in escrow, from the sale of our family home she took $268,000. Violating Federal Rules s.s.322, s.s. 345 and s.s.522, in addition violating Massachusetts non--Bankruptcy Laws. [no administration fees from a residence]

Almost five years have passed from the sale of Malden property and four years from the sale of our home without an accounting of over $688,000 from 34 Mammola way and $400,000 from Triple M. In Malden Ma.This is sheer embezzlement. In addition to Violating s.s.322 fairness to all parties.

The Co--Owners for almost two years have a motion in Judge Feeney's Court to compel Kathleen Dwyer to give a break down is the non-debtors share of rental income, the $400,000 of Malden sale and the $268,000 from 34 Mammola Way sale.

The Debtor's IN Possession's Attorney and Accountant secured a loan of $2,300,000 on September 27 2010. At a cost of $6,000 paid to the Debtors Court appointed Accountant Verdolino & Lowey.

Dwyer refused to use that secured loan, but made sure she paid the accountant his $6,000 for securing the loan. Violating Bankruptcy Code running the business as the debtor has.

Dwyer filed a motion in SRM's Chapter 11 case with respect to $26,000. Owed to the MDOR stating that it was the responsibility of the estate, then another motion stating she had paid $4,400. Yet the MDOR has placed the entire $26,000. Bill on me alone and they have been withdrawing $100 per month out of my social security check. K. Dwyer's final report dated August 22, 2016 she claims ALLOWED AMOUNT IS $4,096.12

Department of Revenue $26,000. What she paid was $4,400 and told R.J.M. if he did not take care of the total amount Judge Feeney would convert the Chapter 11 case to a Chapter 7. I made an agreement with the MDOR for them to take out $ 100 per month from my $805 social security monthly payment. Dwyer stated in Court on 12--16--2014 she was holding $148,000.
Dwyer also in a motion [DOC.305 filed 6-13-2011] stated that the Estate owed these funds.   she would pay the Massachusetts Department of Revenue $26,000.
Kathleen Dwyer, [The Trustee and Debtor withdrew the first amended chapter11 plan in open court 9/27/2011.]

SECOND AMENDED JOINT DISCLOSURE,

>Section D]   Classification and Treatment of Tax Claims
>While the Debtor's liability for the 2009 taxes are not dischargeable by reason of Section 523[a][1][A], the Debtor's liabilities for all three years are also not dischargeable by reason of Section 523[a][1][B].
>Unlike the substantial majority of the other Liam's against the estate, the MDOR claim in its entirety is not dischargeable under Section 1141[d][2] of the Bankruptcy Code.

Dwyer's first meeting with RJM and Diane took place on October 27, 2010 at her offices.

>It was at this meeting Dwyer went over the progress for the sale of Malden, went over the Trust documents and Malden's condo docs. Dwyer was extremely happy with

> the progress and that everything was up to date therefore, did not see this as a difficult or timely situation, and very clear that the any proceeds from Malden to pay off municipal liens in both Revere and Malden would ensure that both income producing properties in Revere would not be in jeopardy and that Mammola way where we resided was a non-issue.

Dwyer confirmed the above with her motions, Doc 134 and 151 with respect to the Private Sale of Malden. More importantly the agreement made with my children prior to the filing of of Doc 134 on December 6, 2010, (where this agreement is referenced) that the taxes in Revere would be paid immediately after the closing of Malden National Grid has attached over $4,000. to my electric bill that she owed at the closing of the Malden sale.

48]. Doc. #580 Filed. 01/ 08 /15 Response of Trustee to Diane Mammola and Michela Mammola's Motion to complete trustee Kathleen Dwyer for an accounting of all funds received and disbursed in the above case. a] Where is the non-debtor's funds $400,000 from Malden Sale. b] Where is the $268,000 from the sale of 34 Mammola Way. c] Where is the balance of the non-debtors 75% monthly rental Income after operational cost 49]. This Court Denied Doc.#539 filed by Interested Parties Diane Mammola, Michela Mammola to Obtain Leave to Sue Chapter 11 Trustee Kathleen Dwyer in her capacity as Chapter 11 Trustee and Individually, and Counsel. Attachments. [cpd]

    a. Motion denied for the reasons stated in the Trustee's Opposition.

Barton v. Barbour,

> But if, by mistake or wrongfully, the receiver takes possession of property belonging to another, such person may bring suit therefor against him personally as a matter of

right, [the receiver would be acting ULTRA VIRES. Parker v. Browning, 8 Paige [N.Y.], 388; Paige v. Smith, 99 Mass. 395; Hills v. Parker, 111 id. 508.

BARTON DOCTRINE, [A] TRUSTEE wrongfully possessing property which is not an asset of the estate may be sued for damages arising out of his illegal occupation in a state court Without Leave of his Appointing Court."]; [The District Court required a motion to be filed in the Bankruptcy Court for leave to sue the Trustee, the Court not knowing the Ultra Vires exception of the Barton Doctrine, and it's clear this Court didn't or just over looked it. As this Court did with Murphy not filing a Proof of Claim for his Fraudulent Claim.]

I'll stop here the injustice goes on and on.

All of the above is what made Seta Rose Mammola's Chapter 11 FAIL,

And by Dwyer violating s.s. 541 that clearly states, co-owned income property is simple. The trustee takes the debtor's share of the income. K. Dwyer took control of 100% of the income. Leaving the co-owners no money to hire ring an attorney, consequently I, RJM had no choice but to fight for myself and my families Constitutional Rights.

I Respectfully, pray this Honorable Court will finally afford me my Right to Due Process under the operation of the law. The First Amendment as is my Constitutional Right by Redressing the Numerous Grievances caused by Judge Feeney, Harold P. Murphy and Kathleen Dwyer. Holding all three accountable for illegally piercing three irrevocable trusts, by going against the "material purpose" of the trust instruments. In addition, revert the trusts back to their original intent. with the principle that preserving the settlor's intent is paramount."

THIS QUOTE OF JUDGE YOUNG IS TAKEN FROM A TOTALLY DIFFERENT BANKRUPTCY CASE. BUT IN MY OPIION ITS PRECISELY WHAT I HAVE WITNESSED IN BOTH MY [RJM] CHAPTER 7 CASE AND MY WIFE [SRM] CHAPTER 11 CASE.

Robert J. Mammola

JUDGE YOUNG'S harshest criticisms were for the LAWYERS involved;

"After 43 years at the bar, the saddest thing about this case is the conduct of the LAWYERS all the LAWYERS. A careful reading of the briefs in this case reveals only a singly recognition that counsel did anything [amiss] in their misrepresentations to the bankruptcy court. Theres blame aplenty, of course. each one blaming everyone else--- including the hapless bankrupt homeowner....... How is it that our profession, the legal profession, --- which could have and should have strongly counseled against the self-interested excesses that set up the collapse-- instead has eagerly aided and abetted those very excesses? How could WE [all of us who profess to be lawyers] have fallen so low.

Robert J. Mammola.   September 20, 2016 Respectfully Submitted,

---

Robert J. Mammola
68 Newton Street
Everett, MA 02149
(781) 844-7933

THE DEAD LINE TO RESPONSE WAS SEPTEMBER 29, 2016

Case 10-15148.   Doc 600.   Filed 10/04/16.   Entered 10/04/16. 16:06:20 Describe Main

MacLean Holloway Doherty & Sheehan, P. C.' S Response to Robert J. Mammola's
"Response to Notice of Trustee's Final Report and Applications for Compensation [NFR]"

Kathleen P. Dwyer, and MacLean Holloway Doherty & Sheehan, P. C., f/k/a MacLean Holloway Doherty Ardiff & Morse, P. C. ["MHD"], as attorney for the Trustee in the above- entitled case, submit TIS response to Robert J. Mammola's " Response to Notice of Trustee's Final Report and Applications for Compensation [NFR]" [Doc. 596].

Robert Mammola is not a creditor in this case and thus lacks standing to object to the Trustee's Final Report and Fee Applications of the Trustee and MHD. See in re Runnels Broadcasting System, LLC, No. 7-02-14217 JR, 2009 WL 4611447, at *3-4 [Bankr. D.N.M. Dec. 1 2009] and in re T.G. Morgan, Inc., 394 B.R. 478 [2008].

Dated: October 4, 2016.   /s/ Kathleen P. Dwyer

                                        Kathleen P. Dwyer BBO #139800
                                        Maclean Holloway
                                        DOHERTY & SHEEHAN, P. C.
                                        8 Essex Center Drive
                                        Peabody, Ma 01960.
                                        [978] 774- 7123
                                        kdwyer@mhdpc.com

The US Constitution, Article VI.2 Clearly states "anything to the contrary notwithstanding", in other words any state or local laws that differ from the original articles and amendments do not override the United States Constitution. All court cases I filed were dismissed in an absolute denial of due process. The Declaration of Independence says, "All men are created equal, that they are endowed by their Creator with certain, unalienable rights." These include substantive due process.

The Supreme Court has developed a broader interpretation of the clause, one that protects basic substantive rights, as well as the right to process. Substantive due process holds is that the due process clause of the Fifth and Fourteenth Amendments guarantees not only that appropriate and just procedures (or " processes ") be used whenever the government is punishing a person or otherwise taking away a person's life, freedom, or property, but that these clauses also guarantee that a person's life, freedom, and property cannot be taken without appropriate governmental justification, regardless of the procedures used to do the taking. In a sense, it makes the due process clause a due substance clause as well.

The district court erred in its ruling.

The bankruptcy judge is protected by absolute judicial immunity for all actions she took in her judicial capacity during the bankruptcy proceeding. Section 455 of Title 28 governs the disqualification of federal judges, including bankruptcy judges from acting in particular case. Of relevance to this particular case are the requirements that a judge shall disqualify him- or herself in "any proceeding in which his or her impartiality might reasonably be questioned" or "where he has a personal bias or prejudice concerning a party" (28 U.S.C. Subsection 455 (a) and (b) (1)).

The trustee defendants must be dismissed for lack of subject matter jurisdiction under the Barton Doctrine, because I did not seek leave of the bankruptcy court. The Barton Doctrine "exception" is when a trustee wrongfully seizes possession of a third party's assets. Property, not assets of the estate, may be sued for damages arising out of his or her illegal occupation in a state court without leave of his or her appointing court (by acting in ultra vires).

Finally, the allegations against the BHF defendants must be dismissed because I based all of my charges against them on statements they made on behalf of clients in the course of litigation. Such statements are protected by the absolute litigation privilege. East Boston Savings bank, through their attorneys committed judicial estoppel. Now the conspiracy scheme of artifice starts to really show the total disregard for any attempt for justice. Judicial estoppel is an inconsistent position of law applied to fact and pure law. (You can't take a position in one court and change your position in another court regarding the same matter.) Their attorney stated in superior court I was a 50 percent owner of all three trusts and repeated that to the Chapter 7 trustee, and then, in a motion in bankruptcy court, stated I was not the owner of record.

The appeals court received an over eight hundred-page brief.

Case no. 13–1801   Date entered March 17, 2014

Plaintiff-appellant Robert J. Mammola appeals the dismissal of his complaint. We affirm, substantially for the reasons articulated by the district court in its memorandum of decision dated May 20, 2013.

They substantially upheld the district court's dismissal but could not have read the eight-hundred-page brief nor the reply brief. Three judges in the pursuit of justice, affirm the district court error. It is a far cry from justice.

> *Rehearing Court*
> *Case no. 13–1801   Entered July 29, 2014*
> *No doubt these judges didn't read the eight-hundred-page brief and reply brief. The case is now successfully filed in the Supreme Court of the United States (Docket 14-68-08), which rules solely on the US Constitution. Thank God.*

> All of the defendants have thirty days to respond. It will be very interesting to see if they are arrogant enough to pull any deceptive legal maneuvering.
>
> The Solicitor General
> November 3, 2014
> The Government hereby waives its right to file a response to the petition in this case, unless requested to do so by the Court.
>
> (Very interesting.)
>
> East Boston Savings Bank Attorney
> October 30, 2014
>
> Dear Clerk,
> Enclosed for filing in the above matter please fined a waiver, on behalf of respondents James M. Liston and Hackett Feinberg, P.C.
> Thank you for your cooperation and assistance.
> Very truly yours, Howard M. Brown

Attorney Brown has listed the respondents to the Supreme Court clerk as (Hackett Feinberg, P.C.). In my writ of certiorari, they are listed "Bartlett Hackett Feinberg, P.C."

"The underlying policy is that all inferior courts and authorities have only limited jurisdiction or powers and must be kept within their legal bounds. This is the concern of the Crown, for the sake of orderly administration of justice, but it is a private complaint which sets the Crown in motion." *Marbury v. Madison*, 5 U.S. 137, 2 L. Ed. 60, 2 L. Ed. 2d 60 (1803).

As Associate Justice James Wilson, the person primarily responsible for the drafting of Article 3 of the US Constitution explains,

In every judicial department, well arranged and well organized, there should be a regular, progressive, gradation of jurisdiction; and one supreme tribunal should superintend and govern all the others. An arrangement in this manner is proper for two reasons: 1. The supreme tribunal produces and preserves a uniformity of decision through the whole judicial system. 2. It confines and supports every inferior court within the limits of its just jurisdiction.

If no superintending tribunal of this nature were established, different courts might adopt different and even contradictory rules of decision; and the distractions, springing from these different and contradictory rules, would be without remedy and without end. Opposite determinations of the same question, in different courts, would be equally final and irreversible.

Consistent with Justice Wilson's explanation, the power to issue writs of certiorari is invested in the highest court of every commonwealth jurisdiction, in some way, shape, or manner. While some incorporate this remedy into their constitutions, e.g., India, others treat it as an implied power of superior courts, e.g., Australia, but in all commonwealth jurisdictions—as distinguished from its American counterpart—it has evolved into a general remedy for the correction of plain error, to bring decisions of an inferior court or tribunal or public authority before the superior court for review so that the court can determine whether to quash such decisions.

US Supplemental Brief per Rule 15.8 November 25, 2014
Regarding Intervening matters not available at the time of filing the partition for a writ.

The following detrimental issues stemming from the trustee in my wife Seta Mammola's Chapter 11 case in relation to the three trust properties. Trustee, Kathleen

Dwyer, appointed by Judge Feeney as a Chapter 11 trustee, which according to Kathleen Dwyer's appointments and her own biography is an experienced Chapter 7 trustee. Upon Dwyer's appointment all bills and check payments were handled through her from October 2010 on.

Some of the bills that she has refused to pay are now causing me serious problems, as referenced in my writ, of constant harassment and embarrassment and now affecting my younger daughter Michela.

A judgment in the Malden court naming me, Robert J. Mammola, as a defendant, All-Tech Electric Inc., the plaintiff. The judgement is in favor of the plaintiff All Tech Electric Inc. for services on the fire alarm system at 10 Yeamans Street Realty Trust property located in Revere, Massachusetts, on June 10, 2011, that Trustee Dwyer was obligated to pay for in the normal course of business while acting as the DIP in Seta's Chapter 11 as the debtor has done with this service company over the previous eight years.

During a previous case where a tenant stopped paying just prior to the bankruptcy, a judge in Malden stated in *Triple M. Realty Trust v. Nestor*, Civil Docket 1250 CV 0325, that only the trustee could recover the approximately $20,000 in arrears owed. That judge in the same court just a year and a half earlier confirmed that once the property was in the bankruptcy court, it was in the hands of the trustee.

Another judgment against me is in Chelsea District Court *Michael Fixman v. Robert Mammola* Doc.12-sc-1073 for services rendered in his official capacity as a constable in March of 2011 through July 2011 in the amount of $1,100 for evictions for the Trust properties.

In both of the above cases, I have received arrest warrants and after those courts finding in favor for the plaintiffs, determining that I owned and was therefore responsible for these bills, despite the numerous documentation that included payments made to each of them from Trustee Dwyer during the same time frame showing that Dwyer had control of the properties and the trust accounts.

The most recent case is against my twenty-four-year-old daughter again in Malden District Court, Doc. 1450SC1957, with a court date of December 5, 2014. This case is in regard to a government grant for lead paint abatement, which was approved on Michela Mammola's property and started. When the job was 95 percent done, the contractor told Michela that the city of Malden is now changing their position due to her being a beneficial owner of Triple M. Realty Trust and that property sold for close to two million ($2,000,000.00) and that the "Mammolas were hiding that money." Trustee Dwyer, in February 11, 2014, which shows in public record, sold the property located in Malden, known as Triple M. Realty Trust, owned by my wife Seta and three daughters, Diane Mammola, Debrah (Mammola) Cenci, and Michela Mammola, each having a 25 percent beneficial interest in all three trust properties. Michela and Diane have brought suit against Dwyer, representing all three girls for a contract they entered into in agreement with Dwyer prior to the private sale of Malden that they would leave their share of the proceeds of approximately $400,000.00 from the sale of Triple M. Realty Trust to pay real estate taxes in the amount of $84,000 to the City of Revere to take the properties out of bankruptcy and if there were monies needed to fund Seta Mammola's

Chapter 11 plan if confirmed, none of which Trustee Dwyer did, and to date, Dwyer refuses to give the non-debtor co-owners their proceeds and has refused a breakdown of the money she claims is gone.

This past Monday, November 24, 2014, Dwyer sent me a copy of two motions filed in Seta's bankruptcy case (standard discharge date of October 2013).

One is an application to employ an accountant and an affidavit claiming she is a disinterested party.

Two is the affidavit of the accountant; the firm Verdolino & Lowey (V&L) were the accountants in Seta's case at the onset, and Trustee Murphy hired the same firm for my Chapter 7 case last year. Again I received my standard discharge December 17, 2010, by Judge Feeney.

Isn't bankruptcy to help with a fresh start? This has left myself and my family destitute, and due to the mishandling of both cases, it is endless. The results of the above are due by the court-appointed trustee Kathleen Dwyer, who stated in a motion filed in the Bankruptcy Court on December 22, 2010, Doc. 151, the property is necessary to the effective reorganization of the debtor. If Trustee Dwyer had followed the original plan that the debtor laid out at the 341 meeting and that the US trustee approved, none of this current disaster would have happened to the entire Mammola family. Today, November 25, 2014, an honorable judge in the Malden, MA, District Court, allowed me to proceed as pro se and indigent on a six-person jury trial dated for March 19, 2015. This trial will give me a chance to prove with documentation that I, Robert Mammola, do not owe the bill in question, regarding All-tech Electric, as a magistrate on November 11, 2014, ruled I was responsible. Kathleen Dwyer with a fiduciary obligation in the shoes of the debtor was obligated to pay these bills, as she was in control of the estate. As a final note, there are three tenants of Triple M. Realty Trust that had deposits to buy their units as condos, which Kathleen Dwyer to this day has failed to refund them, and there is speculation that they are going to initiate court action against myself in light of what is going on. In addition, there is another case in Chelsea, MA, Court, on December 12, 2014 that Constable Michael Fixman is suing me for $1,100 that Trustee Dwyer also did not fulfill her obligation to pay.

Dwyer states she is a disinterest party; she is being sued for breaking a contract, violating Article 1, Section 10., Id re: a contract.

Dwyer violated Fed. R. (1106).

Dwyer violated Fed R. lack of disinterestedness.

The Supreme Court will now rule on the following errors: the district court regarding the Barton Doctrine; Judge Feeney in regard to S.S. 455 Title 28, not giving notice a chance to rise and be heard in open court on record and face his accuser with factual evidence; violation of Civil Right Acts 1983 and 1985; and Murphy on S.S. 1519, violating BHF; and Liston, re: judicial estoppel and S.S. 1519.

Supreme Court Rehearing

Article 1 section 8 clause 4 establishes a uniform rule of naturalization and uniform law on the subject of bankruptcy throughout the United States.

Article 3 of the Constitution—An arrangement in this manner is proper for two reasons:

> The supreme tribunal produces and preserves a uniformity of decision through the whole judicial system.
>
> It confines and supports every inferior court within the limits of its just jurisdiction.
>
> Amendment 1 in part states, "The right of the people peaceably to assemble, and to petition the Government for a redress of grievances."
>
> The Fifth and Fourteenth Amendments detail due process and the equal protection of the law.

Statement of the Case

At the commencement of Seta's bankruptcy filing for chapter on May 11, 2010, the trust properties and family home, the family's holdings, were approximately $12,000,000.00 and had mortgages of only $3,450,000. The mortgages were paid up to date, as they were automatically withdrawn by MTW Bank.

Back real estate taxes and liens going into bankruptcy for both Malden and Revere owed were in the amount of $250,000, with Malden owing the bulk of the liens.

Judge Feeney has a reputation of being fair to all parties and ruled on the facts of the case (see "In re SW Boston Hotel Venture LLC, 449 B.R. 156 (2011)). As I stated at my last hearing on August 6, 2010, when Murphy's allegations started, not long after the transfer of my Chapter 7 case and despite her biased comment about me, my family and I were happy she had both cases and all of the factual documents and therefore would rule on the actual facts. Unfortunately, this was not the case. Judge Feeney's rulings were not based on the facts but on Murphy's allegations, even with the case of a serious conflict of ownership.

Judge Feeney's inability to be impartial and her clear bias against me caused harm not just to me but to my family. We lost everything, even with factual evidence to the contrary of Murphy's allegations, and we were close to being on the street after losing our home.

There is lack of subject matter jurisdiction based upon the Barton Doctrine (28 U.S.C. § 959(a)) because I did not seek leave of the US bankruptcy court, but if by mistake or wrongfully took assets not of the estate "ultra vires."

Murphy repeats whether the district court's dismissal of the complaint was proper as to defendants M and K where I failed to state a claim, which relief may be granted, whether the district court's dismissal was proper, and where I failed to plead fraud with the requisite particularity.

Attorney Lizotte's motion of deception and Murphy's fraudulent claim were based on the motion on whether the district court's dismissal was proper, where my claim was barred as to Lizotte, under the attorney immunity doctrine.

Murphy asked the court to review the manifest of records, which would prove misconduct, lies, and deception, which violated rule 5 of the court.

Murphy, oddly enough, recovered funds on behalf of my bankruptcy estate despite the Chapter 7 filing that listed all assets on July 27, 2010. How did Murphy wrongfully reach into my Chapter 11 without any actual facts? Just as important, why didn't Trustee Dwyer of the Chapter 11 case follow procedure and protect the estate that she had a fiduciary duty to? Better yet, why did Judge Feeney allow Dwyer to break procedure?

This caused the accrual of interest and penalties on the Revere properties' taxes at 16 percent. In turn, on March 14, 2011, the bank was granted relief from stay with respect to 14 Yeamans Street, which was auctioned the first week in April. How was Judge Feeney upholding the integrity of the bankruptcy court and protecting the estate and the parties in interest by ignoring all the factual documentation? Judge Feeney clearly shows her extreme bias toward the appellant with her total disregard for me and the beneficiaries and how her personal bias affected my family.

None of Murphy's or his attorney's motions were questioned, even when cited in my motion of declaratory relief, and every motion filed by me, Seta as Chapter 11 debtor, Diane as appointed manager of Chapter 11, and Michela were totally discarded. Diane, as manager, objected to the first interim fees, especially of Vertolini and Lowey "V&L," since the agreement from the beginning was that Diane would do all of the inputting and information into QuickBooks, saving time, which in turn saved money to benefit the estate. Diane did not take a fee for this, and V&L would not charge for the work Diane was doing. This made everyone in interest happy, as this lifted a large burden off the estate. Yet when the bill from V&L came in at $88,000.00, showing work they did not do, upon a conversation between them and My wife's attorney, my counsel, there would be $14,000.00 taken off immediately and they would go through other charges that should be removed. Diane was given approximately four days to go through the bank and their attorney's bills, Dwyer and her firm's bills, and V&L and their firm's bills.

In spite of that, Diane had found billing errors as stated above with V&L, but Judge Feeney ordered payment of the full amounts on the application fees. V&L got their full $88,000.00.

Murphy states I did not object to the settlement. Appellant's motion for declaratory relief is clearly an objection to Murphy's claim, but his former partner, Judge Feeney, refused to take any action as to my declaratory motion.

What Murphy was not telling the court was that the settlement (*stipulation*) was to allow the private sale of Malden (Triple M. Realty Trust) without Murphy's interference, which would cause Judge Feeney to convert the Chapter 11 to a chapter 7, which would result in the loss of 14 and 10 Yeamans Street to foreclosure and force the sale of the family home because of the time and expense of an adversary proceeding.

The private sale of Triple M. took place at the beginning of February 2011. The beneficiaries were sent the first draft of the stipulation for signature on January 26, 2011, prior to the sale. But this stipulation was not filed until April of 2011. If Judge Feeney had been impartial, the co-owners' proceeds, as directed by them, would have gone to Dwyer to pay Revere's municipal liens with their proceeds of Malden and to fund the Chapter 11 plan.

The limited objection by the bank stated the same, as did the City of Revere's motion to compel, dated February 22, 2011.

Instead of following her earlier rulings that all the parties in interest were in agreement about, she ordered all the surplus proceeds of $400,000.00 from the sale to be held in escrow because of one thing— Murphy's objections based on allegations and lies. Judge Feeney granted the stipulation on May 5, 2011, which at that point should not have been allowed. Judge Feeney had ordered money be held in escrow from the sale, contrary to her earlier order, because of Murphy's allegations, until ownership was decided (civil procedure 12 (b) (6) for failure to state a claim, also Fed. R. Civ. 9(b) failure to plead fraud with the requisite particularly and attorney immunity as to Lizotte).

On October 13, 2010, Murphy filed an application to employ Hanify and King, since renamed Murphy and King. Murphy, Lizotte, and M&K showed total disregard as to "disinterestedness" under the bankruptcy code. The extent of this impact often will be determined by the degree and timing of the disclosure of connection accordingly. The most important rule to remember is disclose and disclose early and often.

None of the defendants disclosed their disinterestedness, even in light of Dwyer, who failed to take any action to prove Murphy's fraudulent claim as trustee for my Chapter 7 case, as the federal rule demands (Bankruptcy Code § 327(a)).

Murphy states, "In fact, Robert Mammola could not demonstrate reliance in any event, since he claimed to have no economic interest in the trust properties that were subject to the settlement motion."

The settlement motion had to do with the private sale of the Malden property for $75,000.00, and if my residence was sold, he would receive an additional 25 percent from that sale.

It is due to Murphy's motions, objections, and claims alleging the trusts are a sham and I had 50 percent beneficial interest. Murphy did not have to prove any of his allegations.

He can't claim I have a beneficial interest in the bankruptcy court and profit from his lies and fraudulent statements that severely augmented the outcome of both my and Seta's bankruptcy estates and then in this court claim that I could not "demonstrate reliance."

Billing for both the bank and Murphy will show many times they looked into piercing the trusts and who the beneficiaries of the trusts were.

Yet Murphy didn't interject after deposing me twice; he waited until the case was in Judge Feeney's court and given her biased opinion, stated it in open court just days after the transfer to her courtroom, opening the door to total disregard for the bankruptcy court and the parties in interest and protecting the assets of the estate turned into enormous administrative fees.

Murphy stated the complaint is largely incomprehensible and laden with Constitution references. This case is based on the Constitution.

Murphy stated I was making unfounded allegations against Judge Feeney, the presiding judge of the RJM Bankruptcy Case. Once again, Judge Feeney, Murphy's former partner, created a bias within Feeney's courtroom about her position. This caused the accrual of interest and penalties on the Revere properties' taxes at 16 percent.

Judge Feeney allowed Murphy to pierce trusts, two of which commenced in 1994, one since 2004, despite the amount of documentation filed in my case and Seta's case, along with EBSB's objection to Murphy stating the properties were owned by the trusts and I was not the owner of record. Trustee Murphy notes that it was the bank that first brought to his attention my undisclosed ownership in the properties.

Regardless, the clear conflict of ownership was now holding up the private sale of the Malden Property because of Murphy's allegations. (See *Northern Pipeline Constr. Co. v. Marathon Pipe Line Co.*, 458 U. S. 50, to suggest that it would be unconstitutional to hold that any and all counterclaims are core. See *Stern v. Marshall*, 546 U.S., 131 S. Ct. 2594

(2011); it could be proven false by material facts that Murphy, Liston, and the court had in its possession the owners of the three trust properties.)

Murphy's objection to the private sale in my bankruptcy was done with tortuous interference and was knowingly false after two depositions of me months prior. Murphy, through Dwyer, forced a settlement between the owners and beneficiaries of the Triple M. Realty Trusts through threats of conversion if he continued this and that an adversarial proceeding would cause the judge to hold the beneficiaries' shares, convert the case, and the two trust properties in Revere and the family home would be gone. Therefore, with the fear of losing both the Revere properties and the possibility of our family home of over twenty-five years, all four women, having no other recourse and believing Dwyer's threats, decided it was in their best interest to enter into a settlement, continuing with the sale that would pay the municipal liens in Revere in full from the three nondebtor beneficiaries' shares.

Motions were being filed in my Chapter 7 case after the December 17, 2010, standard discharge granted by Judge Feeney and then answered in Seta's Chapter 11. The majority of certificates of services did not go out to me, Seta, or the beneficiaries, and when they did, they went to 34 Mammola Way after the sale they forced because of the administrative fees that were growing from the continuances and the fact that Judge Feeney allowed Trustee Dwyer to hold the funds that belonged to the beneficiaries. By agreement, they left them in Dwyer's hand with an agreement that the Revere taxes would be paid, taking the trust properties out of the threat of bankruptcy, despite the fact that they were nondebtors and the only share that would be in bankruptcy was Seta's 25 percent beneficial interest. Due to all of the above defendants' actions, the taxes were not paid. Murphy's objection on January 19, 2011, to EBSB's limited objection motion (Doc. No. 162), dated January 17, 2011, said, "The Trustee should pay from those sale proceeds real estate taxes, water and sewer charges and interest thereon owed in connection with the two Revere properties in which the Debtor (SRM) has an interest." The judge ordered all the funds be held in escrow until he was paid his money ($75,000) and the surplus proceeds (the beneficiaries' share was enough to pay both). Judge Feeney's order, dated January 19, 2011 (Doc. No. 168), granted Murphy's objection. Due to Judge Feeney allowing Murphy's settlement to prevent a lengthy and costly adversarial proceeding that Dwyer said would cost approximately $65,000 and not releasing money that did not belong to the court, 14 Yeamans Street was granted relief on March 11, 2011, one month after the sale of Malden. Then, in April, we were forced to put our residence up for sale because of the administration fees and taxes accruing at approximately $8,000 per month for Revere.

Argument

This suit is based on the US Constitution, the supreme law of the land, the seven articles and the twenty-seven amendments of the United States Constitution, breach of implied covenants, judicial misconduct, and duties of good faith and fair dealing and tortious conduct amounting to intentional misrepresentation, giving rise to violation of M.G.L. c. 93A. Along with the total disregard to the Bankruptcy Reform Act of 1978, to promote the efficiency and to protect and preserve the integrity of the bankruptcy system.

Aforementioned documented facts, motions, agreements, affidavits, and court orders will show defalcation and otherwise effectively causing duress, irreparable harm, and violation of constitutional rights.

The Plaintiff, through factual documentation, attached as exhibits, will show the intent to devise coercion, sabotage, and false representation of claims. In total disregard of Rule 11, as to an attorney statement of facts, the defendants all worked closely together, which is documented in their billing filed in Bankruptcy Court, to accomplish this destruction of a twenty-five-year successful family business.

Robert J. Mammola (RJM) filed Chapter 7 Bankruptcy July 27, 2010. The case was assigned to Judge Hillman's courtroom and the Chapter 7 Trustee Harold Murphy (Murphy).

Prior to the first 341 meeting, August 31, 2010, Andrew Lizotte (Lizotte) of H&K deposed RJM and then again in September prior to the second 341 meeting October 5, 2010, regarding personal finances, SRM's finances, and the trust properties, all original documentation supplied to Murphy at his request.

On September 17, 2010, Doc. No. 15 EBSB filed Relief from Automatic Stay with respect to my properties located at 74 and 80 Meyer Road, Hamilton, MA, and 10 Milano Ave., Revere, MA.

On October 1, 2010, Murphy filed an objection, Doc. No. 17, to the bank's above motion but withdrew that objection in open court on October 13, 2010. This was done three days after Judge Feeney's transfer was signed and less than ten days after Judge Feeney appointed Kathleen Dwyer (Dwyer) "sua sponte" Chapter 11 trustee in SRM's case. One day after Murphy filed for an application to employ and Lizotte filed an appearance in SRM's case, Dwyer hired "H&K," Murphy and Lizotte, as her special counsel in a concurrent, lengthy, and intricate bankruptcy case. Also on October 13, 2010, after the hearing in Judge Hillman's courtroom, order entered at 10:59 a.m., did HBM file an application to employ H&K in RJM's Chapter 7 Case at 1:44 p.m., and Andrew Lizotte (AGL) of H&K filed an appearance in SRM's case no. 10-15148 Doc 115, at 1:46 p.m.

On October 14, 2010, the newly appointed Trustee Dwyer hired Murphy, H&K, as her special counsel in a current, lengthy, and intricate bankruptcy case.

Another conflict of interest in Judge Feeney's courtroom with Dwyer was an adversary hearing filed July 1, 2010, *Dwyer v. Langley et al. Greenberg Traurig*.

Gary Greenberg, shareholder, was the attorney who made the trusts and was our attorney for many years. There are ample documents filed in the Bankruptcy court with Gary's name on it, which Judge Feeney, Dwyer, Murphy, and the bank were very aware of.

In the applications of fees filed in both cases by Murphy and firm and Liston and firm, there are numerous billing times researching the trust documents.

BHF starts as early as 2009.

Murphy and H&K have twenty entries adding up to approximately twenty two hours between October 11, 2010, and September 28, 2011.

That doesn't include the depositions in August and September of 2010 due to the fact there is no record or billing for either because of the material facts that the trusts were valid.

Murphy's objection, filed December 22, 2010, in SRM's case, Doc. No. 149: "In each case, R. Mammola ostensibly utilized his wife, S. Mammola, as trustee and his three children as beneficiaries."

In closing, it's my belief it will prove corruption, nepotism, and despotism in Judge Feeney's courtroom. Judge Feeney allowed Murphy to insert himself into Seta Rose Mammola's Chapter 11 case by using his position as the Chapter 7 Trustee in my case. He did this based on his "theories" and "beliefs." One of his "beliefs" had my wife and I married two years before we met each other and that my two oldest daughters had nothing to do with the trusts and never lived in the family home and claimed the trusts were a sham despite the trust documents being thoroughly examined during my two depositions in his office months before his appearance in my wife's case and just days after Judge Feeney appointed Kathleen Dwyer Chapter 11 trustee in SRM's case "sua sponte."

Judge Feeney used her own personal beliefs against me, Robert J. Mammola, which she made evident in open court with her thoughts through the following statement: "I won't make any gratuitous observations, but I've never thought Seta Rose Mammola was anything but a straw for her husband."

The audacity of a judge to make such a damaging statement about a dedicated husband, father, and businessman in open court just opened the door to her former law partner, who is the trustee in my Chapter #7 bankruptcy case and was made evident in Murphy's claims and false allegations using very similar statements and fraudulent claims in my wife's Chapter #11 reorganization case by claiming I had a 50 percent ownership of all three trusts. The fact is that my wife and daughters each had a 25 percent undivided beneficial ownership from the date of each trust, 1994 and 2004. The trusts that attorney Gary Greenberg made up for my wife, who is twenty-one years my junior, our four-year-old daughter at the time (1994) (I was custodian for her), and my two older daughters was necessary due to my cardiovascular medical condition of atrial fibrillation.

These were not "sham" trusts as Murphy claimed. Murphy and his attorney, Andrew Lizotte, filed on December 22, 2010, Doc.149 in a motion of total lies and deception in Judge Feeney's court. Yet this motion was granted to Murphy. Murphy was misled by BHF, East Boston Savings Bank's attorney Jim Liston, who told Murphy I was a 50 percent owner of the trusts.

The framers of the US Constitution referred to this act usurpation. I filed a motion in Judge Feeney's court, and she simply denied the motion, violating 42 U.S.C. S.S.1985, conspiracy of declaratory relief, and not giving notice an opportunity to be heard.

The bank, through their attorneys, filed their relief from the automatic stay in Judge Hillman's courtroom with respect to the three properties I owned, the two Hamilton properties, and Revere. Milano Avenue was my oldest daughter and her husband's home. The CEO asked for my help when my daughter got sick.

BHF did not file any relief from automatic stay with respect to the trust property in my Chapter 7 until January 7, 2010, after the following took place:

> They were awarded relief from the above three properties by Judge Hillman on October 13, 2010.
>
> Dwyer was appointed trustee in SRM's Chapter11 on October 4, 2010.
>
> Murphy filed an appearance on October 13, 2010.
>
> Standard discharge from Chapter7 on December 17, 2010
>
> Murphy's assertion that the trusts were a "sham" filled in SRM's case.

This started numerous filings in both cases. Motions filed in my case were then answered with objections in SRM's, which led to not being noticed and given proper time if any to object, which led to my filing clarification of declaratory relief in SRM's case in June of 2010 due to the devastation being caused by the BHF, Murphy, Lizotte, and Dwyer going back and forth on who said what while Murphy was using my case to destroy over twenty-five years of family business and pierce trusts that in nonbankruptcy would not have been able to be pierced.

Regardless of any truth or merit to Murphy's claims, Judge Feeney allowed Trustee Dwyer to break procedure and then denied my motion for clarification of declaratory relief for being "procedurally wrong" but granted the motion of deception filed by Trustee Murphy's attorney Lizotte, again despite the factual documentation. Trustee Dwyer, in the same time frame, hired Trustee Murphy and his firm, Murphy & King, as her special counsel, which led to a payment to Murphy's firm of $453,000. This is clearly total disregard for "lack of disinterestedness" and the integrity of the bankruptcy court.

It is my belief that being a prior partner and shareholder of Murphy's firm clouded Judge Feeney's judgment in all further actions or inactions taken there on. By making unfounded and false accusations and questioning ownership of properties, Murphy was trying to create some type of profit for his case. False were the accusations, because months prior, Murphy was already in possession and had full knowledge of all the factual and financial documentation; it is also made very clear in Trustee Dwyer's and Trustee Murphy's billing for fees in the bankruptcy court. The billing shows numerous calls between Dwyer, Murphy, and attorney J. Liston of East Boston Savings Bank.

In Re Persky, 134 B.R. 81 (Bankr. E.D.N.Y. 1991) "that the benefit to the estate of a sale of the nondebtor spouse's right of survivorship is outweighed by the detriment to a family forced to move from its long-term home."

East Boston Savings Bank regarding who the beneficiaries were and "piercing" trusts in October and November 2010.

Judge Feeney allowing Murphy to use his position as my Chapter 7 Trustee through his tortious interference, false claims, and accusations changed the outcome. See *Bartle v. Berry*, 118 F.3d 886 (1st Cir.1997) of the abruptly changed plan that the US trustee approved at the 341 meeting that was well in place by selling Triple M. Realty Trust in Malden as condominiums, this interference led to the taxes not being paid on the two Revere properties, which ended in foreclosure, which then led to the loss of my residence of over twenty-five years due to the costs of the administrative fees.

I have worked very hard and was very successful for my family and myself, and as a family, we acquired $12,000,000 in real estate rental property with mortgages of $3,400,000. Our home was valued in excess of a million dollars, with a mortgage of $270,000. Through the illegal and deceptive actions of Murphy, Lizotte, and M&K, Liston and his firm BHF for the East Boston Savings Bank, and Judge Feeney who allowed an entire family to be displaced, due to all of the above since the private sale of Malden on February 8, 2011, in SRM's case handled by Dwyer,

> I have been taken to court for the closing costs of several vendors that were not paid, along with arrest warrants

> One of the two court cases coming up in Malden is to decide who owned the Malden property and if I am responsible for the payment.

The MDOR is taking $100.00 a month out of my Social Security check for taxes that Dwyer never paid and were filed in SRM's case.

National Grid has added to my personal electric bill $2,450.00 that was owed from the closing of Malden.

The above was to be paid by Dwyer the Trustee in SRM's case, but because of the false allegations this is on me.

The only one who got paid was Murphy, in spite of the motion filed by the US trustee's "limited objection," stating Trustee Dwyer had to resolve the amount that would go to creditors. Trustee Dwyer had other issues, and if a settlement was agreed upon with Trustee Murphy and a plan was filed, then Trustee Murphy would be paid. Nothing was resolved, but Trustee Murphy was paid.

Murphy shows his total disrespect for the US Constitution in a motion dated December 3, 2012, that my complaint is "largely incomprehensible and laden with Constitutional references."

The US Constitution is the best and only contract that the citizens have, and, more important, it's not subject to change for their degree of justice.

What happened to the having a "fresh start"?

I am seventy years old, living in a one-bedroom apartment on the third floor (walk-up) in Malden where these court cases have stemmed from and the business relationships were destroyed.

I have a cardiovascular medical condition called atrial fibrillation, which has been exacerbated, causing other permanent damage and chronic conditions. I had both knees replaced years ago.

Robert J. Mammola

In addition to my income from Social Security of $805.00 per month, less the $100.00 to the MDOR, I receive $180 per month for food from the government.

Dated October 15, 2014

Last Hearing in Judge Feeney's Court
Court Transcript of the Last Hearing

Seta R. Mammola Bankruptcy, 12/16/2014
US Bankruptcy Court, Docket 10-15148-JNF

> MAMMOLA: OK. May I just leave you with this? And I'll stop. Kathleen Dwyer, from everything we've read, and I'm no scholar, all she was in charge of is the debtor's money, 25 percent of all that stuff. She took every nickel. We couldn't afford to hire a lawyer. We cou—didn't have anything. She br—ch—Wha-what did we know? We're in this court. We don't know the laws. And everything we filed here was just shut off, just wouldn't be heard. Tha—
> MAMMOLA: I filed, uh, a-a...
> J: That's not true, sir. I've given you and your family every opportunity—
> MAMMOLA: That's not true.
> J: To address the court.
> MAMMOLA: That is not true.
> J: Uh...
> MAMMOLA: You...I filed a-a declaratory relief. You shut it off before...You wouldn't even—even look a-any part of it. That is absolutely not true. We will file...we'll find out what we're supposed to file and we will file like Your Honor said. Thank you for your time.
> J: And you—you will receive due process, sir.
> MAMMOLA: Thank you.

Seta R. Mammola Bankruptcy, 12/16/2014
US Bankruptcy Court, Docket 10-15148-JNF

J: Uh, these matters are taken under advisement.
DWYER: Thank you.
END OF HEARING

Here is a list of all the court filling that Judge Feeney caused to take place after her last hearing on December 16, 2014, only to have them ultimately dismissed. She said in open court, "Uh, these matters are taken under advisement," and "And you—you will receive due process, sir."

> December 19, 2014—RJM's complaint per Feeney's request
> February 25, 2015—RJM's amended complaint
> February 5, 2015—RJM's response to motion to dismiss
> March 4, 2015—Defendant's motion to dismiss
> March 12, 2015—RJM's response
> April 9, 2015—Feeney's order to dismiss
> April 19, 2015—RJM's motion to extend time to answer
> April 21, 2015—Flannagan's motion for entry of judgment
> April 21, 2015—RJM's motion for reconsideration
> April 24, 2015—Clerk will transmit appeal as assembled by the parties
> April 22, 2015—Feeney's order, request is unnecessary
> April 22, 2015—Feeney's order, there is no authority for plaintiff to answer
> April 22, 2015—Defendant's opposition to plaintiff's motion to reconsideration
> April 22, 2015—RJM's request to wave fee Feeney allowed April 27, 2015
> April 27, 2015—Motion denied, failed to identify any newly discovered evidence
> May 6, 2015—Designation of record and statement of issues
> May 6, 2015—In addition to

June 2, 2015—RJM's response to the order dated May 27, 2015

June 5, 2015—Feeney's order to dismiss after Dwyer elected to move the case to the district court

June 12, 2015—District court notice of appeal reply brief due by July 24, 2015

June 15, 2015—Flannagan's notice of dismissal

June 16, 2015—Gorton dismissal based on appellees notice dated June 15, 2015

July 15, 2015—Motion to reconsider order of dismissal

July 22, 2015—Case opening notice

July 29, 2015—Order of court, appellant by August 12, 2015, show payment of $505, which was paid by Paul V. Mammola

August 3, 2015—Statement of issues and designation of record Judge Gorton dismissal

District of Massachusetts

In Re: Seta Rose Mammola Chapter 7

Debtor	Case No. 10-15148-Jnf
Robert J. Mammola	February 27, 2015
Pro-Se	

Amended Complaint

As the settlor of these trusts and each recorded at the respective registry of deeds, I have an expectancy for the trusts to be followed as intended in the terms of the trust.

The Uniform Trust Code, "UTC" sections 410–417:

"The overall objective of these sections is to enhance flexibility consistent with the principle that preserving the settlor's intent is paramount."

Massachusetts law makes it very clear if in a trust the settlor retains the power to amend, direct the disposition of principal and income, and revoke the trust or any such powers in his lifetime, then the trust is revokable. In short, the settlor has total control. In Triple M. Realty, 10 Yeamans Realty, and 14 Yeamans Street Realty Trusts, the settlor, R.J.M. set up trusts, and pursuant to the terms of the trust has the power and authority to the extent directed by a written instrument signed by all of the beneficiaries and recorded in the Registry of Deeds in Suffolk County.

Party in interest standing is not static across all proceedings within a bankruptcy case; status as a party in interest with respect to some proceedings does not necessarily bestow the same status with respect to other proceedings. Indeed, the legislative history expressly notes that the definition of the term depends on the context of the dispute; a party is not a party in interest with respect to a specific matter unless he or she has a sufficient interest in that matter. This interest may, however, arise as a result of the significance of the issue to the party's rights in the case as a whole. Parties in interest have certain basic rights in the administration and substantive developments in the case. Actions that forever alter a party's rights in the case as a whole—even when the loss of those rights may not alter the party's nonbankruptcy rights in the absence of some future event—nonetheless give rise to an injury in fact; it cannot be seriously questioned that the loss of the protections afforded by the bankruptcy code qualifies as an injury. The preservation of these rights, then, is distinct and personal, not a mere generalized interest in a case or proceeding.

Article III Standing and the Judicial Role

The judicial power is limited under Article III of the Constitution to consideration of cases or controversies. Of course, this limit is a critical component of the tripartite system and a necessary element of any case or proceeding; it may not be waived by the parties or the court. As Chief Justice Roberts once noted:

> It may be worthwhile to recall that the Supreme Court for some time has recognized standing as a constitutionally

based doctrine designed to implement the Framers' concept of the proper—and properly limited—role of the courts in a democratic society. The legitimacy of an unelected, life-tenured judiciary in our democratic republic is bolstered by the constitutional limitation of that judiciary's power in Article III to actual cases and controversies. The need to resolve such an actual case or controversy provides the justification not only for judicial review over the popularly elected and accountable branches of the federal government, but also for the exercise of judicial power itself, which can so profoundly affect the lives, liberty, and property of those to whom it extends.

The Threshold for Injury
"In Regard to Article III"

The majority lowers, at a minimum, the threshold for injury in fact to include anyone who can conjure up the mere risk of a future business impact. The majority's detour from the standard analytic pathway for determining contingent injury ensures that bankruptcy courts will, henceforth, be burdened with determining whether sufficient injury exists among a broad new class of persons who, to obtain party in interest standing, may now allege only a fear that future business dealings with the reorganized entity may result in less profit than projected.

While it is unclear whether the majority decision will have the far-reaching consequences that the dissent predicts, the majority decision certainly invites an expanded notion of standing. It is likely that this decision will be widely cited by parties with tenuous grounds for standing as a basis to be heard in bankruptcy proceedings, at least until such time as the bankruptcy courts have had the opportunity to interpret and apply the majority decision.

The legislative history to 11 U.S.C. S.S. 363(h) indicates that a court should determine whether the benefit to the estate of sale outweighs any detriment to the co-owners of the property, House Report No. 95-595, 95th Cong., 1st Sess. 346 (1977); Senate Report No. 95-989,95th Cong., 2d Sess. 56–57 (1978), US Code Cong. & Admin. News 1978, p. 5787, thus implying that Congress wanted the Bankruptcy Courts to construe broadly the word *detriment* and to take into account not only economic detriment but also the psychological, emotional, and even physical detriment that could result from a S.S. 363(h) sale. "Detriment" therefore means not only economic hardship, but also any loss, harm, injury, or prejudice proximately following from an involuntary displacement. ("Under the Bankruptcy Code, When a House May Not Be a Home," Commercial Law Journal Aug/ Sept 1981 286–289.)

To put it another way, nondebtor's spouse's right to a portion of the sale price will rarely be sufficient to purchase comparable quarters for her and her family. A survivorship interest by itself will not provide a roof to protect the nondebtor's spouse and her family from today's snow and rain. The effect of a S.S. 363(h) sale would be to deprive the nondebtor spouse of two interests, a the possessory and b the survivorship, while compensating her only for the latter.

Studies showing that stressful life events, including relocation, indicate that undesirable events are significantly related to health impairment. Id. at 152 Amendment 1, "Congress shall make no law respecting an establishment of religion, or prohibiting the free exercise thereof; or abridging the freedom of speech, or of the press, or the right of the people peaceably to assemble, and to petition the Government for a redress of grievances."

> The complaint does not allege facts sufficient to support every element of a claim. The court will dismiss the complaint.

I have been and continue to be directly harmed by her misconduct, intentional misrepresentations, and failure to notice me in her motions. Because of her allowing claims and allegations about my ownership without any examination of proof, regardless of all the documentation I had supplied to her in her offices, and ignoring the fact that I had been deposed twice with respect to the trust properties, I suffered the following:

> By ignoring the terms of the trust and taking over 100 percent of the income from the trusts, she stopped paying the bills at 34 Mammola Way, according to the order of the court on a regular basis at first and then stopped paying completely.

> I lost my place of residence and the right at the age of seventy to my retirement and right of survivorship.

> I went months with a chronic heart condition with no health insurance because of her refusal to pay.

> I experienced extreme duress from being forced out of my home with no funds and nowhere to go while watching her do the same to two of my daughters with no means or way to help them, which in turn caused serious health complications that led to additional chronic health problems, landing me in ICU several times while exacerbating my heart condition.

> Because of her misconduct and her handling of the closing of the Triple M. Realty Trust Property in Malden, I have

been dragged into court for bills due by her from the closing. I have received arrest warrants for the same, embarrassment, and the loss of longtime business relationships.

National Grid has attached over $2,000 to my electric bill, which she owed at the closing of the Malden sale.

She filed a motion in Seta's chapter 11 case with respect to $26,000 owed to the MDOR, stating that it was the responsibility of the estate, and then another motion stating she had paid $4,400. Yet the MDOR has placed the entire $26,000 bill on me alone, and they have been withdrawing $100 per month out of my Social Security check.

Her first meeting with Diane and me took place on October 27, 2010, at her offices. It was at this meeting she went over the progress for the sale of Malden, the trust documents, and Malden's condo documents. She was extremely happy with the progress and that everything was up-to-date; therefore, she did not see this as a difficult or timely situation and was very clear that any proceeds from Malden to pay off municipal liens in both Revere and Malden would ensure that both income-producing properties in Revere would not be in jeopardy and that Mammola Way, where we resided, was a nonissue. She confirmed this with her motions, Document 134 and 151, with respect to the private sale of Malden. More important, the agreement made with my children prior to the filing of Document 134 on December 6, 2010, (where this agreement is referenced) confirmed that the taxes in Revere would be paid immediately after the closing of Malden. That took those properties out of tax title, as the mortgages were never late and automatically withdrawn on all three trust properties monthly, which further ensured that our residence of more than twenty-five years would continue to stay out of jeopardy.

She filed a motion in my Chapter 7 case, Document 40, stating that she was actively marketing 10 and 14 Yeamans Street. In direct conflict with her previously mentioned motions filed in Seta's case, neither I nor my wife or children were given notice on these motions to be able to object and show the court these conflicting motions she intentionally filed as she intentionally failed to send notice.

Her intentional misrepresentation directly affected me as well as the beneficiaries.

She did not abide by the binding terms of the trust instrument as the settlor. The trusts were created to benefit my wife and children upon acquiring both Triple M. and 10 Yeamans Street both in 1994.

When I filed Chapter 7, on July 27, 2010, I did not file an exemption in my schedule C because I would remain in the family home, located at 34 Mammola Way, which had been my place of residence for over twenty-five years.

I did not amend my schedule C prior to my standard discharge on December 17, 2010, because of her agreement with my daughters, along with the fact that her conflicts of interest were never disclosed.

Prior to our meeting on October 27, 2010, she had hired the chapter 7 trustee in my case as her "special counsel" in a concurrent and intricate bankruptcy case, which neither ever disclosed until months later while she worked in concert with my trustee, who then made false and unsupported claims that I was a 50 percent owner of the trusts despite all the material facts and the two depositions in Murphy's office. She ignored this.

She did not notice me on any of her filings as required by law.

Her actions of intentional misrepresentation and conflict of interest are in black and white with. The time frame showing conferences with Murphy's counsel regarding the benes and the fact that she ran the title for Mammola Way on December 30, 2010, and called Murphy and counsel with the results show she was working in concert and had no intention of holding up her end of the agreement, following the terms of the trust.

By withholding the money, breaching her agreement to pay the taxes, and using her position with the court to ignore the factual documentation and her obligations as trustee led to the loss of my residence. I had been living there for more than twenty-five years. I also lost my retirement while destroying what I as the settlor wanted for my family. In 1991, I was diagnosed with atrial fibrillation. With my wife being twenty years younger and just having had a child and my two older daughters, who were nineteen and twenty-one, I wanted to ensure they had a future. These trusts were intentionally created so my wife and children would each have a 25 percent undivided interest with rights of survivorship.

She used her position with the court to deny the rights of the beneficiaries with rights of survivorship and as the settlor took total control of the properties and the rights of the beneficiaries. I at no point could amend or change the terms of the trusts or the beneficiaries.

US Bankruptcy Court
District of Massachusetts
Eastern Division

In re: Chapter 7
Seta R. Mammola, Debtor   Case No. 10-15148

Robert J. Mammola   Adv. P. 14-01249
v.
Kathleen Dwyer, et al.

Plaintiffs Response to Motion to Dismiss Amended Complaint

This Honorable Court ordered the Plaintiff to file an Amended Complaint, specifically setting forth his standing to assert claims against the Trustee of the estate of Seta Rose Mammola, as opposed to claims against the Trustee in his personal bankruptcy case, as well as his specific claims for relief, as opposed to those allegedly held by family members whom he cannot represent.

As Ordered by this Honorable Court, the Amended Complaint states that the settlor Robert J. Mammola's expectancy was for the terms and purpose of the trusts by Massachusetts law would be performed per the settlor's intent and material purpose.

The Uniform Trust Code, Sections 410–417

1. Upon Dwyer's appointment as Chapter 11 Trustee in the Seta Rose Mammola case she "stepped into the Debtor's shoes" and to follow the normal course of business as Trustee according to the terms of the trust instruments, which obligated her to non bankruptcy laws as well as federal laws.

The Threshold of Injury in Regard to Article III

"The majority lowers, at a minimum, the threshold for injury in fact to include anyone who can conjure up the mere risk of a future business impact. The majority's detour from the standard analytic pathway for determining contingent injury ensures that bankruptcy courts will, henceforth, be burdened with determining whether sufficient injury exists among a broad new class of persons who, to obtain party in interest standing, may now allege only fear that future business dealings with the reorganized entity may result in less profit than projected."

Attorney Flannagan is very careful to stay away from making any reference to:

Dwyer's actions violated the Uniform Trust Code, section 410–4173

The threshold of injury in regard to Article IV

"The trustee is given legal title to the trust property, but is obligated to act for the good of the beneficiaries. The trustee may be compensated and have expenses reimbursed, but otherwise must turn over all profits from the trust properties. Trustees who violate this fiduciary duty are self-dealing. Courts can reverse self-dealing actions, order profits returned, and impose other sanctions."

The "UTC " makes it mandatory that the settlor's intent is paramount in an irrevocable trust.

Article III states "the bankruptcy court will, henceforth, be burdened with determining whether sufficient injury exists among a broad new class of person who, to obtain party in interest standing, check on proper service any person in a Chapter 11 case has a right to stand and be heard."

Per order of this court the Amended Complaint pertains to injuries that have directly affected me as the settlor of the trust properties, due to Dwyer not following the terms of the trusts created as she was legally obligated. See In re Philip J. Behan. Nevertheless, as the court noted in *Hillman v. Hillman*, 433 Mass. 590 (2001), when interpreting trust language, words should not be read in isolation and out of context; rather every effort should be made to ascertain "the settlor's intent from the trust instrument as a whole and from the circumstances known to the settlor at the time the instrument was executed." Id. at 593.

> Robert J. Mammola, Appellant, v. Kathleen P. Dwyer
> Civil Action No. 15-Cv-11885-Nmg
> As Chapter 7 Trustee for the Estate of Seta Rose Mammola and MacLean Holloway Doherty Ardiff & Morse, P.C., Appellees
>
> **Motion to Reconsider Order of Dismissal**
> This appeal is based on the Adversary Proceeding filed against Trustee Kathleen Dwyer while acting in her

capacity as the Chapter 11 Trustee for the destruction caused by her handling of the Trusts, that I as the Settlor, created in 1994 for my wife and children's future as well as all of our retirement, and how I continue to be harmed by Dwyer's actions.

The defendants in a motion to dismiss asked for documents that show how I have been directly harmed to be stricken from the record, and asked for documents that pertained to my wife's bankruptcy case. With the documents that were a necessary part of my case stricken and documents the defendants asked to be included took the case in another direction stating I did not have standing.

Dwyer ignored the terms of each of the three trusts that clearly state, by her own account, that my wife and three children owned an undivided one-quarter interest in each trust, yet Dwyer took 100 percent control of the income from the trusts, shortly after stopped paying the bills at our family home located at 34 Mammola Way, Medford, MA, despite the order of the court, on a regular basis at first and then stopped paying completely.

Months with no health insurance due to her refusal to pay and with a chronic heart condition

The extreme duress of being forced out of my home with no funds and nowhere to go while watching her do the same to two of my daughters with no means or way to help them, which in turn caused serious health complications and led to additional chronic health problems that landed me in ICU several times while exacerbating my heart condition.

Due to her misconduct and her handling of the closing of the Triple M. Realty Trust Property in Malden, I have been dragged into court for bills due by her from the closing; I have received arrest warrants for the same and the embarrassment and loss of longtime business relationships.

> Dwyer filed a motion in SRM's Chapter 11 case with respect to $26,000 owed to the MDOR stating that it was the responsibility of the estate, then another motion stating she had paid $4,400. Yet the MDOR has placed the entire $26,000 bill on me alone, and they have been withdrawing $100 per month out of my Social Security check since the private sale of Malden on February 8, 2011, in SRM's case, handled by Dwyer,
>
>> One of the two court cases in Malden was to decide who owned the Malden property and if I am responsible for the payment.
>>
>> The MDOR is taking $100.00 a month out of my Social Security check for taxes that Dwyer never paid and were filed in SRM's case.
>>
>> National Grid has added to my personal electric bill $2,450.00 that was owed from the closing of Malden.
>
> The above was to be paid by Dwyer, the trustee in SRM's case, yet were not paid and due to the false allegations and Dwyer telling the vendors when they called for payment that the bills were solely my responsibility.
> As stated in my Amended Complaint, as the settlor of these irrevocable trusts, I placed total control of the

properties and the rights of the beneficiaries. I at no point could amend, change, or revoke the terms of the trusts or the beneficiaries and each was recorded at the respective registry of deeds. I have an expectancy for the trusts to be followed as intended in the terms of the trust.

Prior to receiving the dismissal from this court, I came in to ensure that I was filing correctly now that this appeal had been moved from the BAP to the district court, as I am pro se. It was then I learned after speaking to the clerk that the filings come directly from the bankruptcy court and that both the appellant and appellees could not physically file.

I pray this honorable court will reconsider and afford me my right to due process.

Dated July 14, 2015

The Last Two Filings to the Director, Clifford J. White, III

Clifford J. White, III, Director   August 8, 2016
Executive Office for US Trustee
US Department of Justice, 441 G Street, NW, Suite 6150
Washington, DC 20530

Robert J. Mammola's Response to Mr. Harrington's response to the Debtors Attorney Richard Mistone

Mr. Harrington, the US Trustee for Region 1's Response to the Debtor Seta R. Mammola's Attorney Richard Mestone Complaint dated September 2, 2015. (See Exhibit 1.)
June 3, 2016

Mr. Harrington, the inquiry has been forwarded to me for review and reply. [It never mentioned the mediation resolution exhibit 2 or the affidavit of the debtor's Attorney Richard A. Mestone, exhibit 3]. In my opinion, this affidavit makes it very clear that Annmarie DiGiovanni's letter, dated October 26, 2015, is in total contradiction of the actual facts that transpired in the sale of the property of Triple M. Realty Trust in Malden, Massachusetts, that the debtor Seta Rose Mammola engaged into a contract for a fair market sale [not a broker who would be a part of or just stand by and let a scheme of artifice go (see exhibit 2, 3, and 4].

An entity named the Triple M. Realty Trust ("Trust ") held title to the real estate. Ms. Mammola was the trustee of the Trust and one of four beneficiaries. (At this point, Mr. Harrington learned who the true beneficiaries were, and he had a duty as part of his review and reply to expose Trustee Murphy's fraudulent claim. The document he reviewed clearly showed Robert J. Mammola had no legal ownership in the Trusts.) (See exhibit 5.)

Mr. Harrington states, in his letter dated April 6, 2016, I claimed Mr. Murphy erroneously asserted I maintained an equitable interest of at least 50 percent in the real properties owned by these trusts. Mr. Harrington, in his response, said the It should be UST United States Trustee. Mr Harrington is the Assistant United States Trustee for the District of Massachusetts is responsible for supervising the administration of bankruptcy cases. Had Mr. Harrington done his duty and examined the three irrevocable trusts (see exhibit 5), he would have honored the integrity of the bankruptcy federal rules and charged Murphy with violating F.R. S.S. 1519. (See exhibit 4.) Mr. Harrington's letter of August 5, 2016, makes very clear Murphy's assertions I was a 50 percent owner are erroneous.

Mr. Harrington states Ms. Mammola states that while in Chapter 11 reorganization proceeding, she received an offer to purchase the real estate. It appears, however, that no purchase and sale agreement was ever executed between the parties.

The debtor's attorney, Richard Mistone, was in the process of a What does this stand for? P&S Purchase and Sale agreement on the $2,600,000 offer but was stopped by Judge Feeney's sua sponte appointment of Trustee Dwyer without any just cause or hearing as required by federal rule. Mr. Harrington was very careful not to mention the mediation resolution agreement dated April 13, 2011.

The Mediation Resolution Agreement
Dated April 13, 2011

Through litigation, Century 21 Bond Realty was forced to pay to the original broker, Central Real Estate, a finder's fee because they were the buyers' original broker and signed the offer of $2,600,000 with Seta Rose Mammola, the debtor in possession before Trustee Dwyer was appointed—a finder's fee of $14,250, based on the sale price of $1,900,000 of which the debtor and the co-owners fought with Dwyer over the change in the offer of $2,600,000 to $1,900,000. (Trustee Dwyer took $400,000 less $75,000 to Trustee Murphy. In total disregard to the US trustee's limited objection in regard to Trustee Murphy's payment if any.)

Ms. Mammola did not object to the broker. The debtor in possession hired the same broker in August of 2010. The same broker who worked with the broker of Central Real Estate in regard to the $2,600,000 offer the debtor signed with the ultimate buyers who changed real estate office and broker to work their scheme to lower the $2,600,000 offer to $1,900,000.

When does a buyer's attorney ever get involved in setting the price on property? The debtor in possession already had a signed P/S by both the seller (debtor) who accepted an offer and the buyer who made the offer with a $1,000 deposit. (See facsimile transmittal sheet dated November 11, 2010, from the buyers' attorney.)

> Attorney MeihueHu., Esq.
> November 11, 2010
>
> Dear Attorney Dwyer,
> Here is a version that I advise my client to sign. I will wait for the information as we discussed today from you. Please let me know if there are any final adjustments needed.
> Sincerely, Meihueil Hu, Esq., the Buyers' Attorney

What version on November 11, 2010? An offer of $2,600,000 was signed by both the seller (the debtor in possession) and the buyer on September 25, 2010, with a $1,000 check.

The letter shows total disregard for the US Constitution Article 1, Section 10 regarding contracts, as well as Replace S.S with §by both Attorney Dwyer for the debtor and the co-owners and Attorney Mei Hu, Esq., for the buyers.

The inquiry has been forwarded to me for review and reply. None of the above violations were addressed by Mr. Harrington, who is responsible for supervising the administration of bankruptcy cases and private trustees under Title 11 of the US Code. (Why?)

Mr. Harrington states, "The proposed purchaser was the same buyer who made the previous offer to Ms. Mammola, although on terms different from the original offer." Again, Mr. Harrington omits the scheme of artifice that was played out by the statement of the buyers' attorney.

Attorney Hu violated USC. and S.S. 157.

Congress recently enacted Title 18 USC §157as a companion to § 152. It provides that a person who, having devised or intending to devise a scheme or artifice to defraud and for the purpose of executing or concealing such a scheme or artifice or attempting to do so, files a petition under Title 11, including a fraudulent involuntary bankruptcy petition under Section 303 of such Title 19; files a document in a proceeding under Title 11; or makes a false or fraudulent representation, claim, or promise concerning or in relation to a proceeding under Title 11 at any time (before or after the filing of the petition or in relation to a proceeding falsely asserted to be pending under such title) shall be fined under this title, imprisoned not more than five years or both.

Attorney Dwyer, in her role as trustee in the sale of an irrevocable trust (Triple M. Realty Trust in Malden, Massachusetts) disregarded her fiduciary duty. Article 1, Section 10 of the US Constitution says, "No state shall impair the obligation of contracts."

The Uniform Trust Code states clearly that the duty of a trustee is to act in good faith and in accordance with the terms and purpose of the trust and the interest of the beneficiaries.

Dwyer, without any direction from the beneficiaries, reduced the price of the $2,600,000 offer that was signed by the seller and buyer with a $1,000 deposit to $1,900,000.

Therefore, the attached exhibits were sent to Clifford J. White, the office of the US trustee of the Department of Justice in Washington, DC. They were also sent to the attorney general's office of Boston, Massachusetts. The exhibits will clearly show fraud, conspiracy, and criminal actions by Attorney Kathleen Dwyer, Attorney Meihueil Hu for the buyers, Bond Realty Century 21 of Malden, Massachusetts, and AnnMarie DiGiovanni, all of whom violated my and my family's civil rights.

Mr. Harrington once again omitted my motion dated January 19, 2011, "Objection to the Sale," along with affidavits from the debtor and three co-owners demanding Dwyer sell Triple as condos as laid out and approved at the 341 meeting with the US trustee. (To date, Trustee Dwyer has not paid the tenants their deposits of $23,000 back, which they gave to buy their stores as condos they occupied.)

Mr. Harrington stated accordingly, "These court orders are now final." Not one word of Mr. Harrington's review and reply with regards to Trustee Dwyer violating the section of the court order that spells out that the co-owners were leaving their share to pay Revere's taxes and liens, which Dwyer never did to date, August. 8. 2016.

Exhibit #6

The debtor in possession's attorney and accountant secured a loan of $2,300,000 on September 27, 2010 at a cost of $6,000 paid to the debtor's court-appointed accountant Verdolino and Lowey.

Dwyer refused to use that secured loan but made sure she paid the accountant his $6,000 for securing the loan.

Exhibit 4: Scheme of Artifice.

Criminal Liability for the Bankruptcy Practitioner 311

In *United States v. Sabbeth*, the court of appeals adopted the Gellene Rule 17. The court concluded, "We held long ago that Section 152 is essentially equivalent to a perjury statute and that only basic requirements of perjury need to be proved."

Congress recently enacted USC 18 S.S. 157 as a companion to S.S.152. It provides that a person who, having devised or intending to devise a scheme or artifice to defraud and for the purpose of executing or concealing such a scheme or artifice or attempting to do so, files a petition under Title 11, including a fraudulent involuntary bankruptcy petition under Section 303 of such Title 19; files a document in a proceeding under Title 11; or makes a false or fraudulent representation, claim, or promise concerning or in relation to a proceeding under Title 11 at any time (before or after the filing of the petition or in relation to a proceeding falsely asserted to be pending under such title) shall be fined under this title, imprisoned not more than five years or both.

In addition, the fines for a violation of S.S. 157 can accumulate up to $250,000. Section 157 has two fundamental requirements:

There must be an artifice or scheme to defraud or an intent to devise a scheme or artifice.

The artifice or scheme must be made in contemplation of the filing of a bankruptcy case, the filing of a document in that case, or a representation made to the court in the case.

This is a perfect example of a scheme or artifice.

Sincerely, Robert J. Mammola
August 8, 2016

Clifford J. White, III, Director   August 8, 2016
Executive Office for US Trustee
US Department of Justice, 441 G Street, NW, Suite 6150
Washington, DC 20530

Director White, Sir,

Citizen to citizen, the following factual court-documented injustices will show the total disregard for US Const. Art. I, § 8, Cl. 4., of the US Constitution, the Reform of 1978, the integrity of the bankruptcy rules, and your personal mission statement.

How could the Mammola family, holding $15,000,000 in rental income property, mortgages of $3,450,000, and back real estate taxes due to condo conversion of $250,000 upon my wife filing for Chapter 11 bankruptcy reorganization, owning 25 percent of the above, which offers a "fresh start" yet caused us to lose everything we owned and a family of five to be displaced, especially when the mortgage payments of $23,000 per month were automatically withdrawn on the first of every month for over six years and were never late or missed.

I am writing my response to William Harrington's answer to my initial complaint directly to you, as Harrington has belligerently made it very clear that *cronyism* is alive and well by his blatant disregard of the Reform Act of 1978 and his lack of interest in the integrity of the bankruptcy federal rules.

In Mr. Harrington's response to my complaint, it's very clear his duties to be responsible for supervising the administration of bankruptcy cases and private trustees under Title 11 of the US Code was anything but interested in honoring the integrity of the Bankruptcy Federal Rules or the US Constitution (US Const. Art. I, § 8, Cl. 4. (in part establish standard laws about bankruptcy throughout the United States).

Had he checked Doc.149 filed 12/22/10 p. 2, last line, "Any net proceeds after payment of allowed secured claims may be held pending an adjudication of the respective rights to bankruptcy estates," by investigating would have found a hearing had never taken place due to the relationship of Murphy and Judge Feeney.

Mr. Harrington states I claimed Mr. Murphy erroneously asserted I maintained equitable interests of at least 50 percent in the real properties owned by these trusts. Mr. Harrington in his response [said] the USTP is responsible for supervising the administration of bankruptcy cases. Had he done his duty and examined the three irrevocable trusts (see exhibit 5) he would have honored the integrity of the bankruptcy federal rules and charged Murphy with violating F.R. S.S. 1519. (Also see exhibit 7,

Doc. 149, filed 12/22/10 by Murphy's attorney, Andrew G. Lizotte (A.G.L.) a motion of lies and deception; in part. P. 2 "R. Mammola ostensibly utilized his wife, S. Mammola, as trustee and his three children as beneficiaries.") All trust were irrevocable and recorded at the Registry of Deeds. Trust will show R.J.M. signed all legal documents as custodian for Michela Mammola under the Massachusetts Uniform Transfer to Minors Act (Closing attorney Williams for Mt. Washington Bank caught the mistaken documents that he made up and R.J.M. and S.R.M. signed at the closings but filed at the Registry of Deeds the proper certificate of the true trustee and beneficiaries. P. 3 Trustee Murphy asserts that Triple M. is a sham trust. Attorney Lizotte made this fraudulent statement, knowing that R.J.M. at his deposition supplied all the factual documents that were filed in the Registry of Deeds. R.J.M. also supplied a copy of power of attorney signed by all four beneficiaries. P.4, Attorney Lizotte states, "R. Mammola built the residence on or about 1985. On or about May 13, 1988, R. Mammola transferred the Residence to the Mammola Way Realty Trust. Upon information and belief, S. Mammola and Machela Mammola are the alleged beneficiaries of the trust." Robert and Seta met in September of 1988 and married in May of 1989. Michela was borne August 4, 1990.

P. 5 (16) Attorney Lizotte said, "On or about January 8, 2008, R. Mammola executed and delivered to Mt. Washington Bank a certified personal financial statement. The court documents will show all financial statements were handwritten by R.J.M. The deception above is part of what was supplied to Judge Feeney by Trustee Murphy. As stated many times by Trustee Dwyer, Feeney's personal friend and former *partner*) and Dwyer violated F.R. S.S. 704 (5) proof of claim.

Had Mr. Harrington done his duty and examined my complaint, he would have seen Judge Feeney refused to allow any of my motions or my family's motions and affidavits to be heard. Judge Feeney denied my motion 155 and affidavits of the debtor filed January 19, 2011, violating Title 42, Section 1983 of the U.S.C. It provides that anyone who, under color of state or local law, causes a person to be deprived of rights guaranteed by the US Constitution; today, the Civil Rights Act can be invoked whenever a state or local government official violates a federally guaranteed right). So when Mr. Harrington states there were no objections to the stipulation filed with the US Bankruptcy Court, it is simply not true. (As proof of that, the debtor's attorneys will testify the stipulation was a forced agreement. Attorney Marullo of the debtor (*his words*) stated he was negotiating with Murphy to settle for $10,000. Based on Dwyer's motion filed on December 6, 2010, Doc. 134 that states who the four beneficiaries are who signed the agreement for the private sale of Triple M. In addition, the h will leave their share of $400,000 to fund the debtor's plan, which lays out the payment of property taxes on both 10 and 14 Yeamans St., Revere, MA.

A Bankruptcy Judge Is the Primary Administrator
Rules of Bankruptcy Court

Massachusetts Court System Case and Legal Resources Rules and Orders Supreme Judicial Court SJC Rule 309

Supreme Judicial Court Rule 309: Code of Judicial Conduct The code governs the conduct of all judges and assists judges in establishing and maintaining high standards of judicial and personal conduct (specifically in both the Chapter 11 case of Seta and my Chapter 7 case.).

The code is not intended as an exhaustive guide for the conduct of judges. For example, judges' conduct is also governed by constitutional requirements, statutes, court rules, and decisional law. The code is to be construed so as not to impinge on the essential independence of judges in making judicial decisions. The code is intended to state basic standards that govern the conduct of all judges and to assist judges in establishing and maintaining high standards of judicial and personal conduct.

On July 27, 2010, I filed for Chapter 7 bankruptcy in the Massachusetts Bankruptcy Court in Boston, Case No. 10-1087-Judge Hillman. Harold Murphy was trustee. On May 12, 2010, my wife, Seta Mammola, filed for Chapter 11 bankruptcy in the Massachusetts Bankruptcy Court in Boston, Case No. 10-15148-JNF.

In a billing entry for Murphy and King, dated October 12, 2010, Andrew Lizotte billed (.60) for "Further review of trust documents." With the next billing entry, dated October 13, 2010, he billed (.20) for "Work on notice of appearance in spouse case."

Three months after I filed Chapter 7 and after East Boston Savings Bank's attorney James Liston misled Trustee Murphy by stating I was a 50 percent owner of all three trusts in Seta's Chapter 11 case, Judge Feeney moved my Chapter 7 case into her court on October 25, 2010. If not for justice, then why? Judge Feeney, on October 29, 2010, four days later, showed her true intentions by her biased statement: "I won't make any gratuitous observations, but I've never thought Seta Rose Mammola was anything but a straw for her husband."

East Boston Savings Bank, through the help of their attorney J. Liston and the firm of BHF, very successfully worked their conspiracy plan. They started in Superior Court by making the claim I was a 50 percent owner of all three trusts and then continued the scheme by manipulating Trustee Murphy of R. J. Mammola's Chapter 7 case by making the same fraudulent claim to T. Murphy behind closed doors in October 2010. Then when East Boston Savings Bank was done playing fast and loose with the

Bankruptcy Court, they filed a motion for the court to have an abundance of caution as to T. Murphy's claim.

Attorney J. Liston, in a motion filed in bankruptcy court on January 7, 2011, advised the court to have an abundance of caution as to T. Murphy's veil-piercing and alter ego regarding me being a 50 percent owner of the trusts.

East Boston Savings Bank (EBSB). and Attorney Liston continue by stating I am not the owner of record. (See Petition for Writ p. 17b. Doc 39.) (This was a total contradiction to the position the bank stated in superior court.)

Trustee Murphy, on January 18, 2011, filed a motion stating it was East Boston Savings Bank that first brought it to his attention that I was a 50 percent owner of the trusts.

Judge Feeney had two conflicting motions on her bench and did nothing in pursuit of the truth or justice.

Judge Feeney kept delaying a hearing regarding legal ownership of the three realty trusts, which gave her former partner, Trustee Murphy, all the time needed to force the nondebtors to agree to Murphy's forced stipulation agreement.

Judge Feeney, knowing she ordered Trustee Dwyer to put $400,000 of nondebtors' funds in escrow, pending a hearing regarding the factual ownership of both trusts, had no hearing. But Judge Feeney, six weeks later, gave East Boston Savings Bank (the bank that had their attorney J. Liston blatantly lie to Trustee Murphy as to my being a 50 percent owner of all three trusts) relief from stay on the property at 14 Yeamans Street, Revere, Massachusetts, with taxes owed $14,850. ($400,000 in escrow).

The debtor, Seta, fought with Trustee Dwyer to bring in the attorney who made up the Realty Trusts in 1994. That attorney was Garry Greenberg. What Trustee Dwyer didn't say was that she was in a lawsuit with the firm Greenberg Traurig.

Had Mr. Harrington done his duty and examined my complaint, he would have seen the conflict in the Drumm case and the reason Judge

Feeney, Trustee Murphy, and Trustee Dwyer wouldn't have a hearing on ownership of all three trusts.

On October 14, 2010, the newly appointed Trustee Dwyer hired Murphy, H&K, as her special counsel in a current, lengthy, and intricate bankruptcy case. Another conflict of interest in Judge Feeney's courtroom with Dwyer was an adversary hearing filed July 1, 2010, *Dwyer v. Langley et al.* Gary Greenberg, shareholder, was the attorney who made the trusts and was our attorney for many years. There are ample documents filed in the bankruptcy court with Gary's name on them, which Judge Feeney, Dwyer, Murphy, and the bank were very aware of. In the applications of fees filed in both cases by Murphy and firm and Liston and firm, there are numerous billing times researching the trust documents. BHF starts as early as 2009. Kathleen P. Dwyer was represented by Murphy and King (10-21198 David K Drumm 10-01335, *Dwyer v. Anglo Irish Bank Corporation Limited et al.* Adversary filed 10/14/10, date last filing 08/27/2013).

My response to the order dated May 27, 2015, was postmarked on May 18, 2015, and received on June 1, 2015, with a response time of seven business days of the date of this order.

The court has resolved a dispute as to the designation of record pursuant to Federal Rule Bankr. P. 8009(e)(1) and struck the plaintiff's purported statement of issues. The court affords the plaintiff the opportunity to file, an amended statement of issues on appeal, which properly states the issues presented on appeal from this court's order dismissing his complaint for lack of standing and failure to state a cause of action. This court's order to dismiss dated April 9, 2015, for lack of standing and failure to state any plausible claims for relief against the defendants. This Court has stricken R.J.M. statement of issues and made what this court wants as a statement of issues.

> This court has eliminated any documents that clearly show motions full of misleading and fraudulent claims, deception, and conflicts.

> All of the deception of facts in regard to 10 and 14 Yeamans St. Rt. in regard to the conflicting motions of ownership of the trusts that is clearly stated by Trustee Murphy and the bank's attorney J. Liston. [No action was taken to resolve the true ownership of the three trusts.]
>
> This court has eliminated from the statement of issues any and all factual evidence of Dwyer and the firm's actions that have and continue to cause me harm.

Dwyer completely violated the "material purpose" of the trusts, which were irrevocable.

Mr. Harrington states that I complained that, among other things, Ms. Kathleen Dwyer failed to abide by the terms of the trust instruments. The Realty Trusts are in themselves binding contracts covered by U.S.C. Article 1, Section 10, 1d. Also, as the settlor of these trusts, with each recorded at the respective registry of deeds, I have an expectancy for the trusts to be followed as intended in the terms of the Trust.

The Uniform Trust Code, "UTC" sections 410–417 state, "The overall objective of these sections is to enhance flexibility consistent with the principle that preserving the settlor's intent is paramount."

Massachusetts law makes it very clear that if in a trust, the settlor who retained the power to amend, direct the disposition of principal and income, and revoke the trust or any such powers in his lifetime, then the trust is revocable. In short, the settlor has total control. Triple M. Realty, 10 Yeamans Realty, and 14 Yeamans St. Realty Trusts were set up by me as the settlor.

They are trusts. Pursuant to the terms of the trust, the trustee has the power and authority to the extent directed by a written instrument signed by all of the beneficiaries and recorded in the Registry of Deeds in Suffolk County. (These are clearly irrevocable trusts.)

Mr. Harrington states my perceived conflicts between Mr. Murphy and Ms. Dwyer on, April 5, 2011 (Doc. No. 226, "US Trustees Limited

Objection"). In part, if an agreement was reached, Murphy would not be paid until a reorganization plan was in place. No plan was in place, but Dwyer paid Murphy with nondebtor's funds. Dwyer did not pay the property taxes on the Revere property, per the court approval and allowed per the private sale agreement she signed with the nondebtors in spite of the US trustee's objection and Doc. 134 filed December 6, 2010.

Mr. Harrington states the bankruptcy court dismissed the complaint. A further appeal to the US District Court was also dismissed. The US District Court dismissed the case based on the Barton Doctrine for not seeking bankruptcy court approval. The US District Court Judge Gorton stated, "The plaintiffs may have a legitimate claim for relief against defendants, but unless and until plaintiffs file a motion in the bankruptcy court, seeking leave to file suit and that motion is either granted or denied with leave to appeal, this court lacks jurisdiction and the case must be dismissed." (See Id at 148.)

Judge Gorton, in April 2013, also told Diane and Michela to find a case that stated it was not necessary for bankruptcy approval to sue a trustee—*Satterfield v. Malloy 111*. We concluded that Busch's claims fell "squarely within ultra vires exception to the Barton Doctrine."

The Barton Doctrine applies when a trustee wrongfully possesses property that is not an asset of the estate and may be sued for damages arising out of his or her illegal occupation in a state court without leave of his or appointing court.

In *Spinner v. Nutt* (417 MA), it says, "Beneficiary must show that parties who enter into a contract directly and primarily for the beneficiaries benefit."

July 18, 2013, Diane and Michela filed a motion in bankruptcy court for permission to sue Trustee Dwyer. The motion was stamped in bankruptcy court and immediately brought to federal district court to attain their stamp on the same motion. Seven months later, it was brought to my family's attention by the clerk at the bankruptcy court that the motion to sue was never put onto the docket even though it was stamped as received. The following day, the clerk informed us that she would bring it directly to the records and have it reentered.

On February 12, 2014, we were informed that it had to be put back into a motion form in order for it to be heard. We went on to file on March 20, 2014, for the motion to sue. On the same day, Trustee Dwyer filed an opposition for our motion. Her opposition was granted by Judge Feeney. Judge Feeney wrote, "Motion denied for reasons stated in trustee's motion and opposition."

Judge Feeney erred in her dismissal on the basis of ultra vires exception to the Barton Doctrine. (See exhibit 10, Judge Gorton's Memorandum and Order in exhibit 18, and both motions—July 19, 2013, and March 14, 2014—in exhibit 19.)

Diane and Michela failed to set up a prima facie case on any theory. Exhibits attached to the original suit will show documentation of actual facts, which is a prima facie case.

Trustee Dwyer stated Diane and Michela's claims were "conclusory." The dockets 134 and 151 agreement (contract) in December 2010 are factual evidence. These also became court orders as part of the private sale of Malden property.

As further factual evidence, East Boston's Savings Bank and the City of Revere made motions (2011) for Trustee Dwyer to abide by the agreement made with the co-owners.

The debtor, Seta, on September 27, 2010, secured refinancing through her bankruptcy attorney and the court-appointed accountant in the amount of $2,300,000 at a cost of $6,000. Trustee Dwyer was appointed sua sponte on October 6, 2010 (without any just cause or hearing, as required by bankruptcy code). She refused to use those funds but paid the accountant the $6,000 fee. (Seta insisted Dwyer do so, which would have ended the Chapter 11 case, but Dwyer would not. (Dwyer violated bankruptcy and mass law by taking 100 percent control of all funds, not just the debtor's 25 percent.)

When the property of the debtor is co-owned by a nondebtor, the estate usually succeeds to debtor's rights (n27). Occasionally, however, a trustee may wish to take possession of the debtor's interest in co-owned property. When the property is a commercial or rental real estate property, this may be relatively simple to arrange, with the trustee sharing income from the property.

Dwyer filed in bankruptcy court Doc. 134 on December 6, 2010, in Seta's Chapter 11 case as part of the private sale of Triple M. Realty Trust in Malden, Massachusetts. The agreement that the nondebtors would leave their share of the Malden property ($400,000) to fund the S.R.M. Chapter 11 plan, which would pay Revere's and 10 Yeamans and Fourteen Yeamans Streets' taxes and liens. This agreement was signed by the nondebtors and Trustee Dwyer.

Dwyer filed in bankruptcy court Doc. 42 on January 21, 2011, in R.J.M. Chapter 7 bankruptcy case. The Chapter 11 trustee was marketing the 14 Yeamans Street properties in conjunction with the marketing of the 10 Yeamans Street property, contrary to the nondebtors' wishes in regard to their nonbankruptcy funds of $400,000. (See Doc. 134 and Doc. 151.)

Dwyer took $268,000 from the sale of 34 Mammola, violating state laws and Federal Rule S.S. 522 (a). In addition, Murphy took $25,000.

Spinner v. Nutt (417 MASS) says the beneficiary must show the parties entered into the contract directly and primarily for the beneficiaries' benefit. (See Doc. 134 filed December 6, 2010.)

Section 363 (i) provides, "After a sale of property to which subsection (g) or (h) of this section applies, the trustee shall distribute to the debtor's spouse or co-owners of such property, as the case may be, and to the estate, the proceeds of such sale, less the cost and expenses (not including any compensation of the trustee, of such sale, according to the interest of such spouse or co-owners and the estate).

The following is how an application of CPLR S.S. 5240 affects an S.S. 363 (h) sale.

> In view of state law (construing CPLR S.S. 5240 and the case interpreting that section) and S.S. 522 (b)(2)(B) (sic) of the Bankruptcy Code, there are several reasons

> why courts should not permit trustees to sell family homes held as tenancies by the entirety in New York free of a spouse's interest. First…the debtor's interest remaining in the estate after the operation of section 522 (b)(2)(b) should be a very limited one which extends only to the right of survivorship in the absence of rent. Based upon such a limited right, the drastic remedy of removing a family from their family home should not be available.

The following are conflicts that both Trustee Murphy and Trustee Dwyer had prior to becoming trustees in the two bankruptcy cases. By not disclosing the conflicts of interest that Trustee Dwyer had with the law firm of Greenburg Traurig, both Murphy and Dwyer were able to bypass and break both state and federal laws, rules, and regulations for the courts and the United States Trustee Program. This created a domino effect that continues to cause harm, destroyed a family business, and broke irrevocable trusts, causing the loss of everything I had started and continued with my family to build, which is exactly what the US Trustee Program was put in place to stop (a fresh start).

As of right now, my daughters still have not received an accounting of where money from these trusts has gone and how much has been paid to both Murphy and Dwyer while Dwyer continues to withhold both the funds and the accounting. In fact, Seta's original Chapter 11 case is still open with no activity that we are aware of. It has been open since May 2010. In April 2013, it was converted to a Chapter 7. We have been told that upon closing, there has to be a complete breakdown of the accounting of everything sent to us. To date, July 20, 2016, Dwyer has not responded.

Kathleen Dwyer had two conflicts of interest. The first, which was not disclosed upon learning, at the time, she was appointed in Seta's case she was currently in the middle of an adversarial proceeding with the trust attorney for both 10 and 14 Yeamans Street. Dwyer hired Murphy and his firm, M&K, as her special counsel on or about October 15, 2010, one week after her appointment as Chapter 11 trustee in Seta's bankruptcy case.

On July 1, 2010, Dwyer was plaintiff in an adversarial proceeding with Greenberg Traurig, of which a partner attorney, Gary Greenberg, had made both Triple M. Realty Trust and 10 Yeamans Street Realty Trust in 1994, and the trust documents had his name on them. Both Trustee Murphy and Trustee Dwyer were fully aware of who made the trusts, as they both had all of the trusts' documents.

"Applicants and their professionals must strictly comply with Rule 2014, and the failure to disclose all connections provides a basis to disallow fees and even disqualify the professional" *(In re: Leslie Fay*, 175 B.R. at 533, 536). Indeed, in Leslie Fay, the court noted that the requirements of Federal Rule Bankr. P. 2014 are more encompassing than those governing the disinterestedness inquiry under section 327. For while retention under section 327 is only limited by interests that are "materially adverse," under Rule 2014, "all connections that are not so remote as to be de minimis must be disclosed."

My Chapter 7 bankruptcy case was filed July 27, 2010. When I filed Chapter 7, I did not file an exemption in my schedule C because of the fact that I would remain in the family home located at 34 Mammola Way, which had been my place of residence for over twenty-five years. I did not amend my schedule C prior to my standard discharge on December 17, 2010, because of her agreement with my daughters, along with the fact that her conflicts of interest were never disclosed.

> Dwyer, prior to our meeting on October 27, 2010, had hired Trustee Murphy, the Chapter 7 trustee in my case the week before as her "special counsel" in a concurrent and intricate bankruptcy case, which neither ever disclosed.

Both Murphy and Dwyer worked in concert making false and unsupported claims that I was a 50 percent owner of the trusts, despite all the material facts and the two depositions in Murphy's office, neither of which were ever put on the court docket. Mr. Harrington stated 11 U.S.C. S.S. 704 (a)(1). Right there, Harrington had a duty to examine Murphy's proof of claim per Bankruptcy Code 11 USC § 704(5)

If a purpose would be served, examine proofs of claims and object to the allowance of any claim that is improper." Murphy never filed a proof of claim, breaking bankruptcy procedures, which Trustee Dwyer allowed. She also broke procedure.

Dwyer's actions of intentional misrepresentation and conflict of interest are in black and white with the time frame showing conferences with Murphy's counsel regarding the benes, and the fact that she ran the title for Mammola Way on December 30, 2010, and called Murphy and counsel with the results shows she was working in concert and had no intention of holding up her end of the agreement, following the terms of the trust.

The trustee led to the loss of our family residence, and being displaced at sixty-seven years old from where I had been living for more than twenty-five years, along with my retirement, while destroying what I, as the settlor of the trusts wanted for my family, all of whom had rights of survivorship.

In 1994, we went to one of the top attorneys to create trusts for my wife and children, irrevocable with rights of survivorship, and throughout the years, the same attorneys dealt with matters regarding these properties. Yet, due to these "conflicts of interest" with both trustees, we were told that they could no longer be involved, therefore allowing Murphy to pierce the trusts. In other bankruptcy cases concerning trusts, the "instrument of the trust" and the "settlor's intent" were followed.

Does that mean all trusts in Massachusetts can be discarded if trustees can walk in and take over without abiding by the terms of these trusts? Where does that leave the people who depend on trust attorneys. Bankruptcy trustees can walk in and if, as in this case, the debtor owned 25 percent of these trusts, take 100 percent of the trusts whenever there is a "conflict of interest" in their favor? Trustee Dwyer took 100 percent of the funds of all three irrevocable trust funds, not just the debtor's share.

Lady Justice depicts justice as equipped with three symbols: a sword symbolizing the court's coercive power, a human scale weighing competing claims in each hand, and a blindfold, indicating impartiality.

Justice is a concept of moral rightness based on ethics, rationality, human law, natural law, religion, equity, and fairness, as well as the administration of the law, taking into account the inalienable and inborn rights of all human beings and citizens, the rights of all people and individuals to equal protection before the law of their civil rights, without discrimination on the basis of race, gender, sexual orientation, gender identity, national origin, color, ethnicity, religion, disability, age, or other characteristics.

Sincerely,

Robert J. Mammola

www.ingramcontent.com/pod-product-compliance
Lightning Source LLC
Chambersburg PA
CBHW070245190526
45169CB00001B/310